Smyths of Peasenhall

A Suffolk Dynasty

Leslie Larnder

First edition 2002

© Leslie Larnder 2002

ISBN 0-9537066-1-3

Designed and Printed by
The Lavenham Press Ltd.,
47 Water Street, Lavenham, Suffolk, CO10 9RN.

Acknowledgements

The production of this book would not have been possible without the co-operation and assistance of many organisations and people.

I am indebted to the staff of the Suffolk Record Offices at Ipswich and Lowestoft, the Royal Agricultural Society of England, The Royal Smithfield Club, English Heritage (National Monuments Record), Institution of Mechanical Engineers, Saxmundham library (Suffolk Libraries & Heritage), Suffolk Local History Council, and Strutt and Parker, Ipswich.

On a personal level I wish to thank the following for their assistance and interest; Don Sparrow of Peasenhall and his son Chris, Jasmin Pyemont of Millrise, Peasenhall, Malcolm Burley of Bay House, Peasenhall, Rex Grayston (Formerly of Grayston Bros., engineers, Laxfield), John Wordley of Lorkins Farm, Orsett, Grays, Essex, Robert Malster of Ipswich, Janet Barnes of Kelsale, Saxmundham, Christine Stephenson, and Eddie Baker of Middleton, Janet Gyford of Witham, Essex, Tony Martin of Framlingham, Ann Pilgrim of Bredfield and Sean G Traynor of New Jersey, United States of America.

Many people who have associations with Smyths of Peasenhall have given me photographs, documents, stories, information and their time; I am most grateful to John Levett-Scrivener, Eric Howard, George Howard, the late Raymond Newson, Brenda Newson, Laurie Simpson, Herbert Gardiner, Stanley Paternoster, Olive Borrett, Brenda Pepper, Freda Holmes, and Iris Chilvers.

Lastly, I am indebted to Ruth Paternoster who diligently typed the manuscript and patiently dealt with numerous amendments.

This book is dedicated to all the people who worked at Smyth's or who were in any way connected with the business.

Contents

Acknowledgements i

Contents ii

List of Illustrations iv

Introduction vii

Chapter 1 **The Early Years** .... Page 1
Peasenhall village – arrival of James Smyth senior –
emergence of the "Suffolk Seed Drill" –
"Smyths of Peasenhall" established

Chapter 2 **The Victorian Period** .... Page 4
Death of James Smyth senior –
succeeded by his son James Smyth junior –
coming of the railways to East Anglia –
Witham, Essex factory –
agricultural shows and exhibitions –
depot established in France – overseas trade –
James Josiah Smyth and Herbert Ambrose Smyth's
involvement in the business – death of Herbert
Ambrose Smyth – death of James Smyth junior –
James Josiah Smyth takes the helm – Smyth's become
a registered company – the business prospers

Chapter 3 **The 20th Century** .... Page 24
Difficulties with the French trade – Paris warehouse
vacated – death of James Josiah Smyth – James
Smyth Blackford – Thomas Henry Thirtle – impact
of First World War – economic and agricultural
recession 1920s – Great Depression 1930s –
devastating fire at Peasenhall Works – attempted
buy-outs of the company – agricultural shows and
exhibitions – death of Thomas Henry Thirtle –
succeeded by his son Frank Elven Thirtle – impact
of Second World War – 1950 and 1954 Smithfield
Show – death of Frank Thirtle – business taken over
by local men – introduction of metal drill – business
bought by Ross Group of Grimsby – business closes 1967

Chapter 4 **The Peasenhall Smyths** Page 57
James Smyth senior – James Smyth junior –
Mechanics' Institute – Drill Manufactory
Benefit Society – employee's cottages – village hall –
Peasenhall school board – Peasenhall vicarage –
Peasenhall living – church collections – parish affairs –
obituary James Smyth junior –
Ralph Alexander Mac Smyth – Belle View –
Peasenhall church clock –
"Suffolk Celebrities" Mr Alderman J J Smyth –
obituary James Josiah Smyth – Louisa Ann Smyth

Chapter 5 **Memories of Yesteryear** Page 78
Herbert "Nibs" Denny – the Gardiners –
the Howards – the Paternosters – the Rowes –
Reggie Friend – Raymond "Bunty" Newson –
Mrs Olive Borrett – Fred Burgess – Frank Thirtle

Appendix "A" **Rules of the Peasenhall Mechanics'** Page 87
Institute and Reading Room

Appendix "B" **Rules of the Drill Manufactory** Page 88
Benefit Society

Appendix "C" **Key Dates** Page 92

Bibliography Page 93

List of Illustrations

1	A peaceful scene in The Street Peasenhall.	Page 1
2	A scene from the past. A posed photograph of a team of four fine horses pulling a seed drill. *SRO Ipswich SPS2357*	Page 4
3	An early advertising poster	Page 10
4	Another early poster aimed at the French market	Page 12
5	The cover of a German catalogue of 1865 *SRO Ipswich*	Page 14
6	An illustration from the 1865 German catalogue. *SRO Ipswich*	Page 16
7	Employees of the Peasenhall Drill Works, plus donkey, 1880.	Page 18
8	Illustration from an early 20th Smyth's catalogue. *SRO Ipswich HC23/E3/1*	Page 21
9	Blacksmiths shop at Peasenhall Works. *SRO Ipswich HC23/E1/1*	Page 22
10	A Smyth seed drill made by craftsmen. The photograph was taken in the yard of the Peasenhall Works with the company offices and foundry chimney in the background. *SRO Ipswich HC23/E6/7*	Page 27
11	Illustration of the Paris depot from a 20th Smyth's catalogue. *SRO Ipswich HC23/E3/1*	Page 29
12	The Peasenhall Works shown on an Ordnance Survey map revised in 1903. The Hall, Le Chalet, Assembly Room and Mechanics' Institute are also depicted. *Ordnance Survey Office*	Page 31

13	An aerial photograph of the extensive Peasenhall Works.	Page 34
14	The scene of devastation at the Peasenhall Works as a result of the 1923 fire.	Page 38
15	This photograph illustrates the intensity of the 1923 fire.	Page 38
16	Photograph of James Smyth & Sons exhibits, Royal Agricultural Show, London (Park Royal). *SRO Ipswich HC23/E1/1*	Page 47
17	Smyth's stand at an agricultural show between the wars.	Page 48
18	*From left to right* Thomas Henry Thirtle, Fred Woodard, Herbert Paternoster and Charlie Howard at the Suffolk Show at Saxmundham during the 1930s.	Page 48
19	A gathering of the Peasenhall workforce to celebrate the wedding of Frank Thirtle 15 July 1935.	Page 52
20	The Peasenhall workforce enjoy a bottle of beer to celebrate Frank Thirtle's wedding on 15 July 1935.	Page 53
21	The obelisk memorial to James Smyth jnr. and his wife Mary Ann in Peasenhall churchyard. A former Smyth's building forms the backdrop.	Page 58
22	Peasenhall Hall built in 1846 by James Smyth jnr.	Page 59
23	The building formerly used as the Mechanics' Institute can be seen on the left of this old photograph of The Causeway, Peasenhall.	Page 61
24	Peasenhall village hall, formerly the Assembly Room, built by James Josiah Smyth for the benefit of the people of Peasenhall.	Page 62
25	Belle View the Victorian home of James Josiah Smyth.	Page 70

26	Photograph of James Josiah Smyth from "Suffolk Celebrities". *SRO Lowestoft*	Page 73
27	The fine memorial in Peasenhall cemetery which marks the final resting place of James Josiah Smyth and his wife Louisa Ann.	Page 75
28	Example of James Josiah Smyth's signature. The value of the cheque equates to about £85,000 at today's value.	Page 76
29	Charlie Howard in 1911 when he was chauffeur to the Collett family who lived at Peasenhall Hall. The photograph was taken at the Ancient House, Peasenhall.	Page 79
30	A job well done by Stanley Paternoster a Works blacksmith.	Page 81

Introduction

East Anglia contains some of the most fertile and productive land in England earning it the epithet "The bread basket of England". Because it is a region whose economy for the last two hundred years or more has been largely based on agriculture, it may not be surprising that it found itself at the forefront in the invention, pioneering, and development of agricultural implements and machinery.

Suffolk in particular was a major centre of the agricultural implements and machinery industry from the time when mechanisation was introduced into agriculture. From the latter part of the 18th century until towards the end of the 20th century a number of leading manufacturers were based in the county from where they gained a national and international reputation for their innovative and high quality products.

Foremost among the Suffolk manufacturers were Ransomes of Ipswich. Robert Ransome in 1789 moved from his premises in Norwich to set up a foundry in Ipswich where he established a business that over time grew into an engineering empire employing at one time several thousand workers. During the earlier part of their history Ransomes manufactured a wide range of agricultural implements but it was the plough which became their forte as a result of case-hardening the ploughshares thereby greatly improving the wearing qualities of the cutting edge. They later introduced interchangeable plough parts making it possible to replace worn parts in the field. Thus adding to their pre-eminence in the production of ploughs.

Ransomes went on to make fixed and portable steam engines and later diversified into the manufacture of railway materials, vehicles and grass cutting machinery and also launched into civil engineering. The firm still operates today under the name of Ransomes, Sims and Jeffries Ltd. but on a very much reduced scale from the days when Ransomes were regarded as an engineering giant.

Garretts of Leiston were another legendary Suffolk firm. Their origins were similarly based on the manufacture of agricultural implements which from a small beginning developed into a major business employing many local people.

It is said that Garretts were formed in 1778 when the first Richard Garrett having started with a blacksmith's shop and forge, subsequently expanded into a major business employing at its peak a workforce of over 2000 and Leiston grew around the factory.

Garretts made seed drills, chaff cutters, ploughs and reaping machines as well as other implements and they were pre-eminent in the manufacture of threshing machines. In later years they expanded into building steam tractors, road locomotives, steam rollers and wagons and eventually electric and motor vehicles. During the First World War they even made small aircraft and, in the Second World War, guns for merchant ships.

The company experienced a financial crisis in 1919 and were forced into a merger with a number of other firms to form a consortium. This itself went into Receivership in 1932 when the Garrett business was purchased by a Manchester firm. Further changes of ownership occurred in 1976 and 1980 and in 1985 the business closed bringing to an end a long and proud history of iron-founding and large scale engineering in Leiston.

As remarkable as is the history of both Ransomes and Garretts, neither Ipswich nor Leiston are the focus of this story but the village of Peasenhall. It was here in 1800 that James Smyth set up his seed drill business. This lasted for more that 150 years dominating the village both by its physical presence and in providing employment for generations of local men, and earning a reputation for their products that remained virtually unrivalled for more that a century.

Peasenhall not only benefited from the employment opportunities that the firm provided but also from the benevolent influence of the Smyths. Evidence of their generosity, social responsibility and visual impact on the village remains to this day.

Chapter 1

The Early Years

The village of Peasenhall nestles in a valley between the neighbouring villages of Yoxford and Dennington in east Suffolk where the surrounding undulating terrain with an abundance of trees creates a picture of rural England at its best. Peasenhall is an ancient place as there was a settlement here in Roman times if not before and for centuries past local people have utilised the land and made a living from it. The core of the village lies either side of the main road that runs side by side with the brook and presents a scene that is largely unchanged within living memory and before.

1 A peaceful scene in The Street Peasenhall.

Peasenhall can lay little claim to fame; Sir Charles Tennyson, grandson of Lord Alfred Tennyson the renowned poet, in the 1930's lived in the Ancient House and, sadly, two of his sons Frederick Penrose and Charles Julian Tennyson are commemorated on the local war memorial having lost their lives in the Second World War.

Charles Henry Collett in 1933 served as Lord Mayor of London having lived in Peasenhall earlier in his life. His father, Henry Collett, bought the Hall in 1892 when the house came on the market following the death of James Smyth junior, and the Collett family lived there until 1926.

The Early Years

The village in 1902 came to national prominence in circumstances that it would not have wished when a young servant girl Rose Harsent was brutally killed in the house where she worked in what became nationally known as the Peasenhall Murder. Coincidentally, the local man, William Gardiner, who was twice tried for the murder and acquitted, amidst much national publicity, worked at Smyth's as a foreman carpenter.

It is in Peasenhall that the story of Smyth's unfolds.

1 The *East Anglian Daily Times* of Saturday, July 6th 1901 featured an article entitled *"New East Anglia - The History of the Suffolk Drill"* which article forms the basis of the early history of "Smyths of Peasenhall". Around the turn of the 18th century James Smyth, a young man from Sweffling a village a few miles from Peasenhall, set up a wheelwright's workshop *"on the north side of the main road leading from Peasenhall Street to Framlingham"*. His work included the repair of the seed drills in use at that time known as Norfolk block drills which had a number of inherent shortcomings. James Smyth formed an association with a Peasenhall farmer Robert Wardley who occupied Grove Farm opposite the wheelwright's workshop.

With his encouragement and financial assistance, much time and effort was spent to improve the drill locally then in use.

Although crude seed drills had been used by earlier civilisations in India, China and elsewhere, in England it was not until early in the 18th century that a rudimentary drill was introduced by an English agriculturalist Jethro Tull which enabled seeds to be sown mechanically. The seed drill brought an improvement to the broadcast system of seeding as it placed the seed below the soil surface in parallel rows of sufficient space to allow hoeing to be easily carried out. Tull's early drill was but the fore-runner. Later in the 18th century improved drills were introduced until at the end of that century the drill commonly used in Suffolk was the type known as the Norfolk drill.

James Smyth's endeavours were rewarded in 1800 when he produced a modified and more effective implement that would become known as the "Suffolk Drill". The first step had now been taken in a business that would continue for more that a century and a half. This would result in "Smyths of Peasenhall" becoming synonymous with agricultural drills and renowned throughout the country and many parts of the world for the quality and reliability of their products.

At this point it would be as well to make passing reference to James Smyth's younger brother Jonathan; he served an apprenticeship as a wheelwright with James in Peasenhall before eventually returning to Sweffling where he established his own business making drills. The business was carried on by his son Joshua who proclaimed in one of his advertising posters that he was the *"......son and successor to the original inventor and maker of the Suffolk Improved Lever corn, seed and manure drill, Sweffling, Saxmundham, Suffolk. Established 1815."*

1 Suffolk Record Office (SRO), Ipswich

Despite Joshua Smyth's claim that his father Jonathan was the inventor of the Suffolk improved lever drill it is far more likely that this drill was pioneered and introduced by James Smyth. It is undeniable that while in the 19th century the Peasenhall business grew into a large and flourishing firm with a world-wide reputation, the Sweffling business remained small employing only a few people and is believed to have closed early in the 20th century.

Having produced an improved implement James Smyth had to set about marketing it at a time when communications and means for advertising were very limited; James Smyth was not only a good wheelwright, he was also an entrepreneur. It is recorded that, having introduced some of his drills into use locally, he recruited some trustworthy men, instructed them in the use of the drill and sent them around the country where they stood in various markets offering to drill at the price of 2s.6d. an acre. These early salesmen were given a £5 note to start with on the understanding that this would be repaid by instalments out of the profits they made. Land-owners and farmers seeing the obvious benefits of the improved drill purchased their own and "Smyths of Peasenhall" were established. The small wheelwright's workshop on the road to Framlingham became inadequate as business in the manufacture of drills expanded and James Smyth re-located to a site in Church Street, Peasenhall where the firm would remain for more than 150 years.

Chapter 2
The Victorian Period

Queen Victoria was born in 1819, came to the throne in 1837 and died in 1901; she reigned over an empire that comprised a quarter of the earth's surface and a third of all its people, an empire on which it was said "the sun never sets". The Royal Navy ruled the seas and during her lifetime Great Britain came to the height of its power and influence. London was the commercial and financial capital of the world.

The Industrial Revolution started in Britain in the second half of the 18th century. British capitalists during the following century made Britain into the world's leading industrial nation based on industries such as coal-mining, iron and steel, chemicals, ship building and engineering. The country was rich and prosperous although the prosperity was not shared by all its people and many lived in appalling conditions judged by today's standards. The change from an economy based on agriculture to an industrial based economy created a massive population movement from the country to the towns and the population of Britain grew from less that 9 million in 1750 to around 45 million by 1911, a fivefold increase. The many additional mouths had to be fed and the need to maximise the use of arable land by increasing yields was a motivating force in encouraging the invention and introduction of new and improved agricultural implements and machinery.

2 A scene from the past. A posed photograph of a team of four fine horses pulling a seed drill. SRO Ipswich SPS2357

Unlike most of his rivals who tended to manufacture a variety of agricultural implements, James Smyth, having pioneered a major improvement in the design and performance of drills, specialised in this particular implement. By the time of his death in 1843 his drill had earned an enviable reputation and was being purchased by farmers, agriculturalists and others in various parts of the country including wealthy landowners and members of the nobility.

James Smyth was succeeded as the head of the firm by his son James Smyth jnr. and an advertisment he produced in 1840 throws some light on the earlier years of the business and extracts from it are reproduced below:-

2   *1840*

CORN, SEED, AND MANURE DRILL, & THRASHING MACHINE MANUFACTORY,

ESTABLISHED IN 1800

AT PEASENHALL, NEAR YOXFORD, SUFFOLK.

————oooooooo————

JAMES SMYTH, Jun.

RESPECTFULLY informs Noblemen, Gentlemen, and Agriculturists in general, that he is sole proprietor of the above establishment, formerly conducted as the firm of SMYTH & SONS, and having had twenty years experience in the business with his Father and for himself, takes this method of soliciting a continuance of that liberal patronage so long evinced towards him, and of the preference shown to his improved LEVER CORN DRILL.

J.S.JUN. having made some very recent improvements to the Drill, now claims unusual attention from Agriculturalists, particular to that appertaining to the Cog Work for DRILLING UNEVEN SURFACES, which not only adds to the appearance of the Machine, but is of the utmost utility in its operations, causing the Cog Wheel on the Barrel that deposits the seeds to work in a central position over the Cog Wheel on the nave, when either ascending or descending a HILL, which was never before accomplished by any other Maker!

The newly invented Additional Box fitted upon Corn and Manure Drills for drilling seeds between the rows of corn at the same time the corn is drilled, is also highly approved by many eminent Agriculturalists who have had them; and it forms a very light Machine when fitted on the frame by itself for drilling seeds only.

J.S.JUN. begs to acquaint the Public that he continues to conduct EVERY BRANCH of the business under his own immediate superintendence, and that his DRILLS are warranted to be made of the very best and choicest materials and workmanship, and on very simple, complete, and approved principles; and by confining his entire business to the manufacturing of DRILLS, only, and from his very extended trade, he is enabled to supply his friends with a very superior article at the reduced prices specified below.

2 SRO, Ipswich HC23/E5/3

Upwards of two thousand two hundred Corn and Manure Drills having been manufactured at this Establishment, within the last forty years, which having given universal satisfaction, J.S. hopes will be considered as entitling him to public patronage, and assures those gentlemen who may favor him with their orders, that his best attention shall be given to the execution of them. And he begs his friends will be particular in giving all the information possible of the description of land, whether light or heavy; and if very strong, the width of the stetches or ridges, or if ploughed to broad flat-work, whether the land, be very flat or very hilly, particularly if side-hilly; the quantity of each description of grain or seeds usually required per acre, and the width they wish the rows to be apart, particularly beans and peas. Also for MANURE DRILLS, it is right to state the kind of manure likely to be used, width of rows apart, and the quantity per acre. The more information he receives the better he will be able to judge of what will be likely, best to suit those who may oblige him with their orders.

This authentic advertisement clarifies and confirms a number of important points in the history of Smyth's; firstly, there is confirmation that the business was established in 1800; secondly, that in 1840 James Smyth jnr. (the son of the founder) was the sole proprietor (at the age of 33 years) before the death of his father (who died in 1843 aged 66 years) and he had worked in the business since he was 13 years of age; additionally, the statement that *"Upwards of two thousand two hundred Corn and Manure Drills having been manufactured at this Establishment within the last forty years....."* (in other words from when the business was founded) provides clear evidence that the product had proved to be satisfactory and had been marketed successfully.

The advertisement also included a list entitled *"The following is a reference to a few of the Persons for whom Orders have been executed"* and included *"His Grace the Duke of Rutland; his Grace the Duke of Newcastle; his Grace the Duke of Leeds, and his Grace the Duke of Portland."* The extensive list specified numerous people in the counties of Middlesex, Norfolk, Lincolnshire, Rutland, Northamptonshire, Huntingdonshire, Cambridgeshire, Hertfordshire, Oxfordshire, Gloucestershire, Berkshire, Hampshire, Sussex, Surrey, Kent and as far afield as Shropshire. The list for Suffolk was headed by The Rt. Hon. the Earl of Stradbroke, President of the East Suffolk Agricultural Association, and the Rt. Hon. Lord Huntingfield and included A. Manning, esq; Messrs. White, Wardley, Baldry, Girling, Lay, Kerridge, Baker, Row, Wade and Hurren of Peasenhall.

The long and impressive list of clients illustrates the significant progress Smyth's had made since 1800 and they were now established as a leading maker of drills.

The reference at the top of the advertisement to *"THRASHING MACHINE"* is puzzling and is contradicted by the statement that James Smyth jnr. has confined his entire business to the manufacture of drills only. This is the only reference that the author has seen to Smyth's making thrashing machines and there is overwhelming evidence that they concentrated virtually solely on the development, improvement and manufacture of drills and for which they were pre-eminent.

It will be noted that James Smyth jnr. (hereafter referred to as JS jnr.) stated in the advertisement that *".....he is enabled to supply his friends with a very superior article at the reduced prices specified below";* the list of prices was headed:- *"List of Prices for Ready Money or a Bankers acceptance at Two Months"* and by way of example of the reduced prices a *"New Drill with 9 rows, 2 corn barrels and rappers"* was priced for 1840 at £21.15s. whereas prior to 1814 it cost £34 and a *"New Drill with 15 rows, 2 corn barrels and rappers"* was £29.5s. and £46 respectively.

JS jnr.'s explanation for the reduction in prices sounds plausible but it should be recognised that there was intense competition in the agricultural implement sector with names such as Garretts of Leiston, Ransomes of Ipswich, Hornsby of Grantham and Coultas also of Grantham, and many other smaller firms all making various types of drills. No doubt Smyth's sought to keep and extend their share of the market, not only by the excellence of their products, but by also offering competitive prices.

The considerable distances that some of the drills had to travel to reach their destination raises the question of transportation before the advent of railways. Probably some were simply drawn by horses or loaded onto horse-drawn heavy waggons to make their way by road or track to the place of use; it is known that Smyth's drills for the southern counties were dispatched by coasting vessels from Aldeburgh to London and then by sea to a more local port; it is likely that drills destined for Cambridgeshire, Norfolk and Lincolnshire went directly from Aldeburgh to small ports such as Kings Lynn, Wisbech or Boston.

The coming of the railways greatly improved the means of transport in Britain and in East Anglia the final section of the Eastern Counties Railway Line from London to Colchester was opened for passenger traffic on 29 March 1843. The Eastern Counties Railway's original scheme was to serve East Anglia by a line from London to Yarmouth and Norwich via Ipswich but in the event their line reached only as far as Colchester and another company, the Eastern Union Railway, was formed with the objective of extending the line from Colchester into Suffolk and Norfolk via Ipswich. Construction work began in October 1844; the line from Colchester to Ipswich was completed and opened for goods traffic on 1 June 1846. The Ipswich, Norwich and Yarmouth Railway proposed to construct a line from Ipswich to serve east Suffolk to Bungay and it was not intended for the line to pass through Saxmundham but take a route about five miles west through Peasenhall.

JS jnr. was a keen supporter of the proposed railway, which he could see would bring economic benefits for his business, and he appeared before a Parliamentary Committee to give evidence in favour of it. He told the committee that he found it economical to dispatch his drills for London by road as far as Witham, Essex from where the rail freight charge was eight shillings per ton (many of the drills weighed half a ton or more) whereas if the drills were put on a train at Colchester the Eastern Counties Railway charged twenty-five shillings a ton. However, the line from Ipswich was routed through Saxmundham on its way to Halesworth and the station nearest to the drill works was to be at Darsham some four miles distant.

Witham's location on the Eastern Counties Railway line must have proved attractive to JS jnr. for he decided to establish a branch of the business in the town no doubt to gain easier and cheaper access to London for his drills. While information on the Witham branch is limited, it is known from Kelly's Essex directories that Smyth's operated there from around 1850 (the year 1844 is quoted elsewhere) until 1895 or 1896 and during the whole of this time a Peter Hannar acted as agent and manager.

The 1851 census for Witham shows that Peter Hannar and his wife were born in Suffolk and indeed both of their children had been born in Peasenhall which supports a view that he left the Peasenhall works to manage the Witham operations. He is described in the 1851 census as *"Drill manufacturer employing nine men"* (this description changes in the 1861 census to *"Manager for drill manufacturer"*). The 1851 census also reveals an influx of other Suffolk men and families with Peasenhall connections and, as most of the nine men named below also lived near the Witham drill factory and their trades are associated with that industry, it is likely that they also left Peasenhall with Peter Hannar to set up the Essex branch of the business:-

John Ship	*Painter*
James Warden	*Blacksmith*
Robert Cocksedge	*Painter*
William Brown	*Carpenter*
James Howard	*Blacksmith*
Charles Clark	*Sawyer*
Nathan Hayward	*Sawyer*
Stephen Lummis	*Carpenter*
James Newby	*Blacksmith*

There is evidence to show that in 1860 Smyth's bought premises in Newland Street (now 126-128) Witham together with some land behind and, as the 1851 census shows Peter Hannar living there, it could be presumed that Smyth's had rented the premises prior to 1860. In 1860 the premises were described as *"All that formerly known as the Blue Posts Hotel but now converted into a drill manufactory and managers and foreman's residence, range of buildings comprising workshops, smith's shop and iron warehouse with ware rooms and lofts over, the same two yards covering together with the site of the buildings excluding the chase half an acre."* JS jnr. and his son James Josiah Smyth sold some of the site in 1871 and James Josiah sold the yard (in later times referred to as the "Drill Yard") in 1896 by which time it seems that operations had come to a close.

Smyth's presence in Witham during the second half of the 19th century coincides with the business reaching its peak when more than one hundred men and boys were employed in Peasenhall, advertising posters proudly proclaimed the extent of their empire *"James Smyth & Sons Peasenhall, Suffolk, England. Branch Establishments Witham, Essex; & Rue Lafayette, 160. Paris",* and their drills were being exported to many parts of the world.

In common with other agricultural implement manufacturers, Smyth's exhibited at various shows and exhibitions from the middle of the 19th century as this was a good means of displaying their products to a large number of potential customers in what was a very competitive market. The Royal Agricultural Society of England (RASE) was founded in 1839, Smyth's became members in 1840. The catalogue for the Society's show *"of the various agricultural implements, machines and other articles for farm purposes, etc."* at Exeter in 1850 includes reference to *"James Smyth of Peasenhall, Yoxford, Suffolk, and Witham, Essex";* they were allocated Stand No. 63 and the twelve articles displayed were all drills of one type or another ranging in price from *"Article No. 6- A Patent Manure Drill; invented, improved and manufactured by the exhibitor. This drill has for its object the most efficient method of drilling compost, or other damp or dry manure, with or without seeds, and that a portion of soil may cover the manure before the seed is deposited, and has a patent apparatus for the regular seeding hilly land etc. Price £37.15s."* to *"Article No. 12 - A two-rowed Turnip Seed or Mangold Wurtzel Northumberland Rowl Drill; improved and manufactured by the exhibiter. This drill is constructed of cups instead of brushes, thereby causing an accurate delivery of seeds, with a knowledge, by cog wheels, for certain deposit of any quantity required per acre. Price £8.10s."*

The prices may seem remarkably cheap but at today's values £37.15s. equates to approximately £1850 and £8.10s. to around £420 which puts the prices into perspective!

Smyth's for many years exhibited at the Smithfield Show and the catalogue for the 1864 Show held at the Royal Agricultural Hall, Islington, London contains the following information:-

The Victorian Period

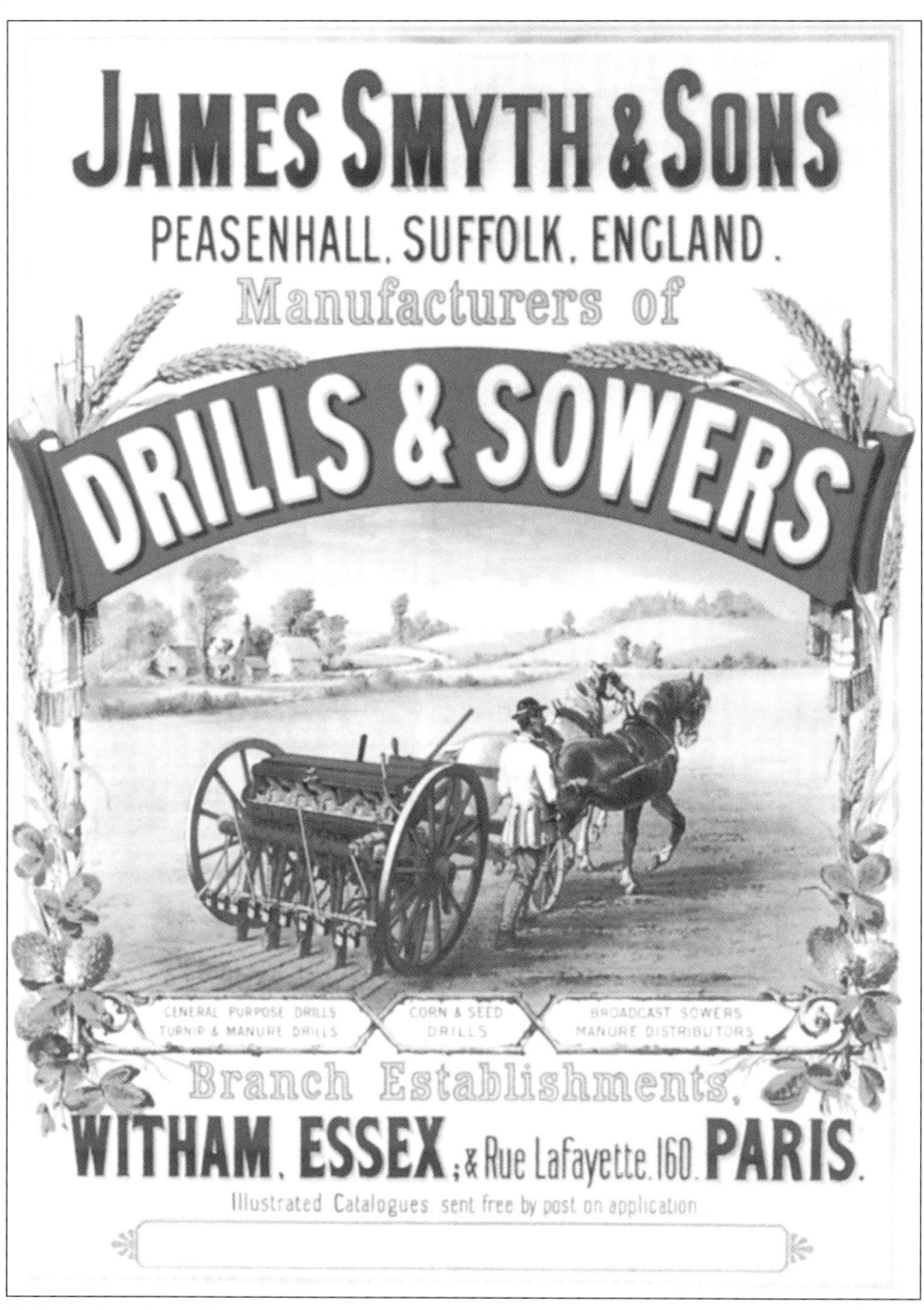

3 An early advertising poster.

"Stand No. 165.- James Smyth & Sons, Peasenhall, Suffolk and Witham, Essex.

	£.	s.	d.
Patent Telescopic Lever Corn and Seed Drill fitted with carriage, steerage, and Broadcast Clover and Seed Box	33	5	0
Patent Telescopic 10-row and Lever Corn Drill	25	15	0
Fourteen row and Lever Corn Drill	30	15	0
Turnip Mangel Wurzel Seed and Manure Drill	29	0	0
Kaemmerers Patent Broad-cast Corn or Seed Sowing Machine	15	10	0"

Smyth's not only exhibited in England but such was their confidence in their products and the desire to trade in the international markets that they also involved themselves in exhibitions overseas and their letter heads indicate that, in addition to London 1862, they won International Exhibition Prize Medals in Vienna 1873, Paris 1867, 1878, 1889, 1900. Sydney 1880, Melbourne 1881 and Amsterdam 1883.

An undated advertising poster most probably produced early in the 20th century pronounced with due pride that James Smyth and Sons, Ltd. Peasenhall Suffolk, England had won *"122 Gold & Silver Medals & Other Awards."* The medals were depicted and many had been awarded at expositions in different regions and cities of France (Compeigne, Reims, Amiens, Nancy, Arras, Soissons, Laon and others) and in Belgium, Germany, Norway, Austria, Australia and Ireland.

The importance of their overseas business can be seen from the fact that during the second half of the 19th century they leased premises in France to serve as a base and outlet for Europe. The *"Directory of Suffolk with Great Yarmouth 1868"* by Morris records under the heading *"Peasenhall Trades and Professions; Smyth James and Sons, Inventors, Patentees, and manufacturers of the original Suffolk drill; and at Witham, Essex and Dieppe, France."* Little is known of the Dieppe depot but the catalogues of the Smithfield Club Shows (later the Royal Smithfield Club) indicate that Smyth's first exhibited at the Shows in 1862 and the 1868 catalogue describes Smyth's as *"James Smyth and Sons, Peasenhall, Suffolk; Witham, Essex; and 17 Rue Magnan, Paris;"* the 1878 catalogue refers to them having premises at 160 Rue Lafayette, Paris, by 1887 they were at 65, Rue d'Allemagne, Paris and finally in 1892 they had moved to 65, Rue Philippe de Girard 8, Paris where they remained until 1907. It is unlikely that manufacturing occurred in Dieppe or the various Paris premises but rather that they were warehouses for the storage of assembled drills and spare parts for distribution to different regions of France and possibly elsewhere on the continent. A Smyth's illustrated catalogue of 1899 includes an illustration of the premises in Rue Philippe de Girard 8, Paris and describes it as a *"Continental Depot"* which

The Victorian Period

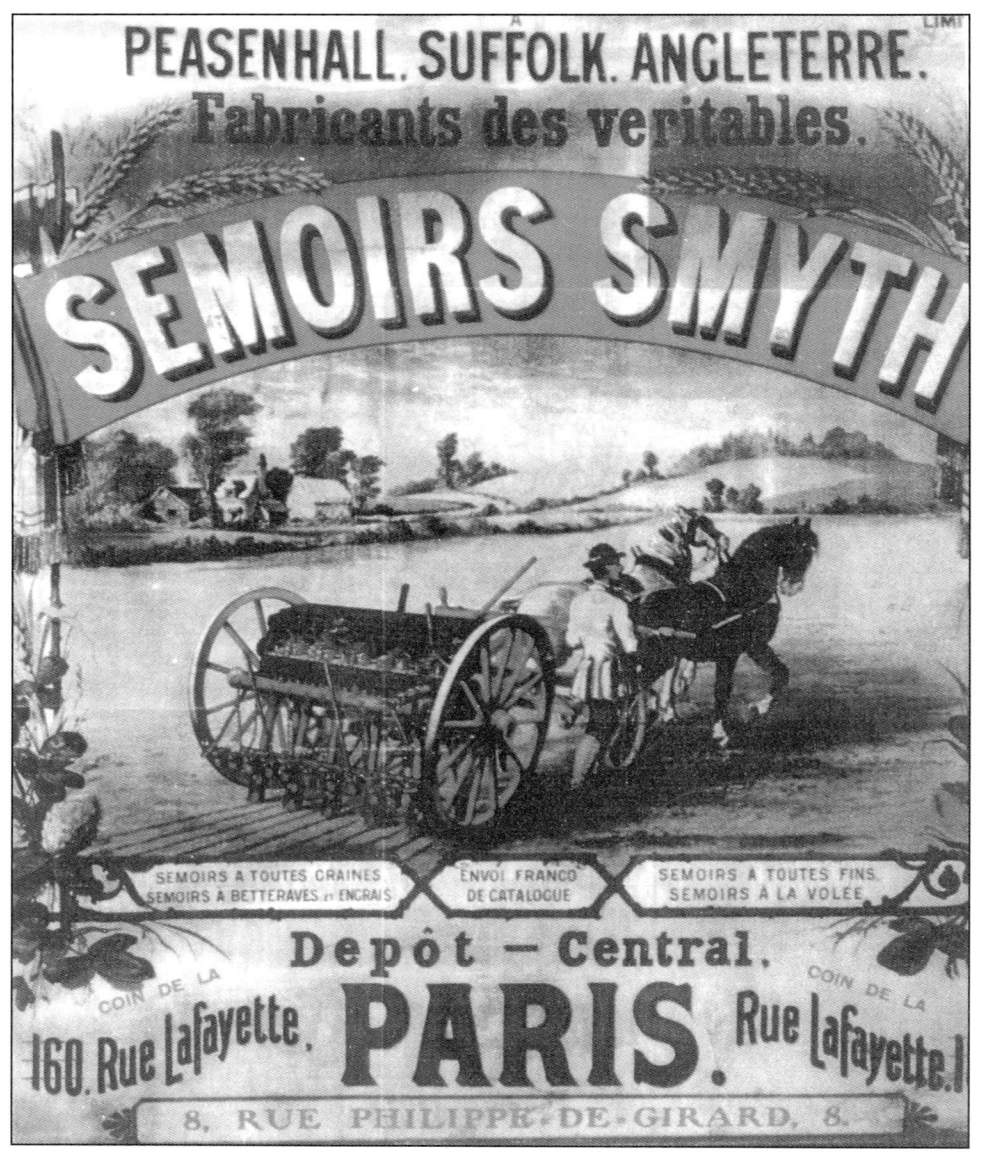

4 Another early poster aimed at the French market.

supports the assumption that it was used to also serve European countries other than France. An undated coloured advertising poster in French refers to the Central Depot being at 8, Rue Philippe de Girard 8, corner of Rue Lafayette so it seems that the two different addresses were one and the same premises.

Among the valuable Smyth archives held in the Suffolk Record Office, Ipswich is a notebook entitled *3 "Measurements & Weights of Drills, Sowing Machines As Packed For Shipment"* and which typifies the remarkable detailed records kept by the Smyths particularly during the 19th century. The note book contains details of Destination, Description of Drill etc., Distance between Rows, Name of Consignee or Sender, Order Book Number, Measurements, Cubic Feet, Nett Weight and Gross Weight, it covers the period from 21 August 1877 to 5 January 1898 and gives details of 127 drills or other implements. The list of destinations is astonishing including, as it does, Sydney, Canterbury (New Zealand), Lisbon, Odessa (Russia) (the consignee or sender in this case was Ransomes Sims and Co.), Volo (Greece), Madrid, New York, Constantinople (now Istanbul) Turkey, Montevideo (South America), Santiago (Chile), Bombay, Naples (Italy), East London (South Africa), Rio de Janeiro (Brazil), San Francisco, Whitewood (Canada), Buenos Aires (Argentina), and Algeria; the place names quoted do not form an exhaustive list but are used to illustrate the incredible extent that Smyth's drills were in demand and give credibility to the claim that they were used throughout almost the entire world.

The foreign and colonial trade was particularly important during the last quarter of the 19th century as a world economic depression was experienced and Britain suffered from a prolonged agricultural recession that retarded home business. It has been said that at the turn of the century at least half of the Smyth's business came from overseas trade achieved in the face of competition from other manufacturers including Ransomes and Garretts who also had developed foreign markets.

JS jnr. had built on the legacy handed on by his father and under his leadership the business continued to be successful notwithstanding periods when trading conditions were very difficult. As well as securing the success of his business on a day to day basis JS jnr. was astute and far sighted enough to prepare for the time when he would no longer be at the helm. He ensured that two of his sons, James Josiah and Herbert Ambrose, were suitably groomed to provide continuity of the business in the future including the education of James Josiah in Germany. The 1851 census shows James Smyth as head of the family, aged 44 years and described as a *"Commercial seed manure drill manufacturer";* his wife was Mary Ann aged 25 years; James Josiah, Son, aged 17 years and described as *"Drill manufacturers clerk";* There are details of other children including Herbert Ambrose aged 13 years, scholar.

3 SRO Ipswich HC23/E1/1(e)

5 The cover of a German catalogue of 1865. SRO Ipswich

So as early as 1851 James Josiah Smyth was working in the business and being prepared for the time when he would become head of the firm. Little is known about Herbert Ambrose; however, in 1950 a number of pupils from Peasenhall school visited "the Works" (as the factory was known locally) and each wrote an essay about Smyth's based on what they had seen and what they had been told by Mr. F E Thirtle (Managing Director) and Mr. Fred Rowe (Company Secretary).[4] They would have been familiar with the history of the firm and some of its personalities as this was passed by word of mouth from one generation to another. One pupil wrote *"James Smyth jnr. had his two sons educated in France and Holland* (undoubtedly this was a reference to James Josiah and Herbert Ambrose); Another pupil wrote *"then he (James Smyth jnr.) had a son called James Josiah Smyth and he went to school in Germany to be educated to take on the business. Then Josiah and Herbert Smyth travelled all over Europe taking orders for drills."* Another recorded *"James Smyth started in a little carpenter's shop. It was not big enough so he started the Works, that was in 1800 then when he died it was Herbert and Josiah Smyth who took over. It was then James Smyth and Sons Ltd. Herbert went abroad and learnt the foreign languages. Josiah then was making drills."* Another source of information regarding Herbert is the publication *"A Survey of the Agriculture of Suffolk"* by P J O Trist (County Agricultural Adviser, Suffolk) 1971, which states *"In the latter years of James Smyth senior a successful export business had been set up and, following his death in 1843 his son James gave two of his sons a special training in this expanding part of their trade.*

James Josiah Smyth travelled northern Europe and his brother Herbert, France and Belgium."

Incontrovertible evidence is provided in a letter of 15 December 1904 from James Josiah Smyth to a Mr Gower in which he said *"Mine has indeed been an eventful life, thanks to my bringing up. My father did wisely in making us boys go abroad to learn foreign languages and then to throw us on our own resources expecting us to show something in return for what he had spent upon us. I to attend to Holland, Germany and Austria; and my brother Herbert to attend to Belgium France and Spain. The result was that for many years my journeyings brought much business from the German speaking nations, and my brother established a good business in France."*

There is little doubt that *"us boys"* means James Josiah and Herbert Ambrose and it is evident that JS jnr. prepared the two sons for the time when he would no longer be in charge and they were made well aware of the vital importance of the foreign trade particularly in Europe.

The status of the two sons within the business is explained in a formal[5] agreement of the 28 March 1864 between James Smyth, James Josiah Smyth and

4 SRO Ipswich HC23/12/1   5 SRO Ipswich

6 *An illustration from the 1865 German catalogue. SRO Ipswich*

Herbert Ambrose Smyth; the agreement is a lengthy document expressed in a legal manner which does not make for easy reading or explanation but it does make clear that *"....James Smyth and James Josiah Smyth have for some years past carried on the Trade or Business of Drill Manufacturers at Peasenhall aforesaid, and at Witham in the County of Essex, and at Dieppe in France."* The document reveals that in effect seven eighth parts of the business were held by James Smyth and one eighth part by James Josiah Smyth as copartners and the principal object of the agreement was to assign one of James Smyth's seven eighth parts to Herbert Ambrose Smyth thereby making him a copartner in the business. The agreement dealt also with the question of salaries and profits as follows:-

"It is hereby declared and agreed that each of them the said James Smyth, James Josiah Smyth and Herbert Ambrose Smyth, shall and will at all times during the continuance of the said Copartnership use, employ and devote their respective attention, industry, and diligence to the conducting, managing, carrying on, improving, and extending the said Trade or Business for the mutual benefit of

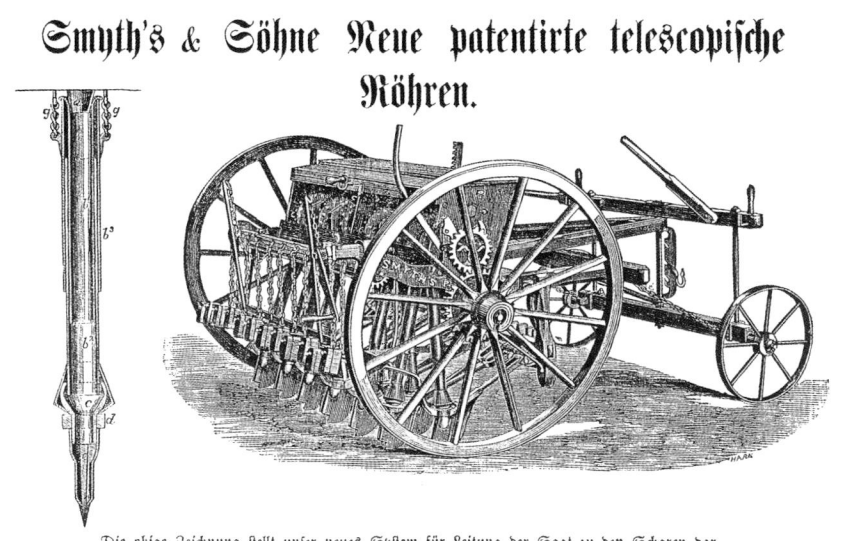

themselves, each of them receiving out of the aforesaid partnership profits or funds, the following salaries, videlicet the said James Smyth the sum of Two hundred and fifty pounds per annum (£11,500), the said James Josiah Smyth the sum of Two hundred pounds per annum (£9,200), and the said Herbert Ambrose Smyth the sum of One hundred and fifty pounds per annum (£6,900), for such their respective services, And subject to the payment thereof, and subject as hereinbefore mentioned, All the income and profits arising from the said Trades or Businesses, shall from time to time during the continuance of the said partnership, be divided between them the said Copartners in the following shares or proportions, videlicet, the said James Smyth Six eighth parts or shares, the said James Josiah Smyth One eighth part or share, and the said Herbert Ambrose Smyth the remaining One eighth part or share thereof." (Today's approximate values are shown in brackets).

"The sting in the tail" for the two sons was that, while they were entitled to share in any profits of the business, they also had an obligation on a proportional basis to bear any losses and pay the salaries, wages, taxes, rents and other expenses of the business. The agreement illustrates the astuteness of James Smyth Jnr. and ensured that his two sons were fully motivated to put their energies and abilities into the business both for their own personal benefit and the future prosperity of the firm.

However, Herbert Ambrose Smyth's involvement in the business appears to have been short-lived as, whilst he is included in the 1861 census as living with his brother, James Josiah, he is not mentioned in the 1871 census or in any other relevant documents after the 1864 agreement and it is believed that he died between 1864 and 1871.

JS jnr. died in 1891 and the business passed to his eldest son, James Josiah, whom it will be seen had been managing affairs since 1857 and who was well prepared for taking the business forward into the last phase of its existence with a Smyth at its head.

The Smyth's attitudes toward commerce and of keeping abreast of technological developments in their field of operations are exemplified by James Josiah Smyth's membership of the Institution of Mechanical Engineers; he was elected a Member in 1882, the proposal form having been signed by R C Ransome, Frederick Turner and Richard Rapier (all well known names of the time associated with engineering in Suffolk) states:-

"Mr James Josiah Smyth served his time with his father at Peasenhall some 7 years (partly at the carpenter's bench, partly as fitter and latterly in office and out of doors duties) and since 1857 partner and manager."

James Josiah Smyth (hereafter referred to as JJS) was invited to prepare a paper entitled *"On Machinery For The Sowing of Seed"* (April 1882) and present it to a meeting of the Institution; the paper, as might be expected, is comprehensive and

The Victorian Period

7 Employees of the Peasenhall Drill Works, plus donkey, 1880

to reproduce it in its entirety would serve little purpose but there are parts of the paper that are of historical value and a number of these are set out below:-

"Corn and Seed Drills - In preparing this paper the writer was anxious to introduce the most improved existing examples: he however deems it not out of place to exhibit before the members a working model of the Suffolk Drill constructed by his father in the year 1838; which will at least serve for comparison, and thus make apparent the advance which has since been attained. Fig. 23, Plate 42, represents the present type of Suffolk Corn Drill; and Figs. 27 to 29, Plates 44 to 46, the writers latest "Nonpareil" design On reference to Fig. 27, Plate 44, it will be seen that a drill is composed of-

1. *A seed-box with its seeding apparatus;*
2. *A frame mounted on two high travelling wheels, the latter furnished with cog gearing for driving the seeding apparatus;*
3. *Levers with the accompanying coulters, by means of which the seed is deposited in the soil;*
4. *Conductors, which convey the seed from the seeding apparatus to the coulters;*
5. *Apparatus for guiding or steering the drill."*

"3 The coulter-levers are a main and important feature in the modern drill. Previous to the adoption of the lever system (which originated with the so-called "Suffolk Drill"), all the coulters were fixed in one transverse beam; whereas in this system each coulter is fixed to an independent lever."

"Abstract of Discussion on Machinery for Sowing Seed".

"Mr Smyth exhibited a model of the early Suffolk drill, made forty years ago by his father, who was now in his seventy-fifth year, and was unable to be present in consequence of illness."

"The lever system however was pretty much as it had descended from his grandfather in the year 1800, when he made the first Suffolk lever drill; and it remained so to this day."

"The PRESIDENT said he was sure the thanks of the members were due to Mr Smyth. They would agree that he had almost exhausted his subject, and had brought it forward in a very clear manner. He could not help saying that Mr Smyth's criticisms on other makers had also been fair and candid. They had also to thank him for the numerous diagrams, which it appeared he had drawn himself with his own hand."

Coming as they do directly from JJS the above extracts clarify that the lever system had descended from his grandfather (James Smyth died 1843) in 1800 when he made the first Suffolk lever drill and they also give a definitive description of a seed drill. Smyth's drills were described in the early days as the "Suffolk Drill", followed later by the "Eclipse" model and then most famously the "Nonpareil" referred to in the paper.

The Victorian Period

The fact that JJS was invited to present a paper to the members of a respected technical institution reflects the high standing and reputation that Smyth's held in the world of seed drills where they enjoyed a position at the leading edge of the technology at that time.

The approach of the end of both the 19th century and the Victorian period saw Smyth's in good shape and, despite the difficult home trading conditions brought about by the agricultural depression of the last quarter of the century, the business was probably at the height of its prosperity and about 100 workers were employed at this time.

A good indication of the progress that had been made can be seen from the increased number drills being manufactured; according to the advertisement of 1840, which has been referred to previously, 2,200 had been manufactured since the formation of the business in 1800 which averages 55 per year or a little over one drill per week; *6* an illustrated catalogue of 1899 claims *"22,000 of our Drills already sold"* and if the 2,200 drills are subtracted from this figure then 19,800 drills were made between 1840 and 1899, an average of 335 per year or almost 6.5 drills per week, a remarkable achievement.

A significant change in the status of the business took place in 1893 when a *7* formal agreement was entered into by James Josiah Smyth which resulted in Smyth's becoming a registered company and JJS no longer having sole ownership and control of the business; the capital of the new company was £25,000 divided into 500 shares of £50 each of which shares numbered 1 to 350 were allotted to JSS (valued at £17,500 or £962,500 at today's value) together with a number of redeemable debentures. The 500 shares was a nominal number and in fact 352 shares of £50 each were issued; receipts in respect of dividends paid in 1893 show the 352 shares had been divided as follows:-

James Josiah Smyth	208
The share holding in 1896 was reduced to	187
Ralph Alexander Mac Smyth (Brother of James Josiah Smyth)	100
The share holding in 1896 was increased to	121
Louisa Ann Smyth (Wife of James Josiah Smyth)	10
Sarah Caroline Blackford (Sister of James Josiah Smyth)	6
Mary Ada Madeline Smyth (Sister of James Josiah Smyth)	11
Aimie M Beatrice Garrett (Sister of James Josiah Smyth)	4
(She signed the 1897 receipt Aimie M Beatrice Smyth)	
James Robinson Garrett (Husband of Aimie M Beatrice Garrett (Smyth), one time Vicar of Peasenhall and later Rector of Helmingham Suffolk)	2
Monsieur Maraval (He was Smyth's Paris Manager)	11
Total Shares	**352**

6 SRO Ipswich HC/E3/1   7 SRO Ipswich HC23/C1

The Victorian Period

JAMES SMYTH & SONS, Limited, Peasenhall, Suffolk; and Paris (Rue Philippe-de-Girard).

PATENT "NONPAREIL" CORN DRILL.
(Acknowledged throughout Europe as the most perfect Drill in the Market).
The Result of 100 Years' Progressive Experience.

8 Illustration from an early 20th Smyth's catalogue. SRO Ipswich HC23/E3/1

With the exception of M. Maraval all the shares were held by Smyth's or people connected with the family and the controlling interests were firmly in the hands of JJS and Ralph A M Smyth although more radical changes were not too far off.

Further evidence of the company's achievements can be seen from the dividends paid to shareholders following the 1893 agreement; the total amount of dividends for the year ending 31 December 1893 paid to JJS and the six other "family" shareholders amounted to £2,557 free of income tax (£140,635 at today's value) of which £1,560 (£85,800) was paid to JJS himself. The total amount of dividends for the year 1892 to 1897 inclusive paid to the same seven shareholders was in the region of £6,816 (£374,880) free of income tax. When it is realised that in 1899 a corn drill could be bought from Smyth's from between £25 and £38, depending on the type and size, the scale of operations and the number of drills sold to enable substantial profits to be generated, are clear to see.

The company entered the last decade of the 19th century with strong demand for their implements and a glance at *8* Order Book "G" covering the period 24 March 1890 - 22 December 1891 discloses the popularity of their drills locally, nationally and on the continent.

In the immediate locality drills were delivered to W B Barham and I M Yetts (both of Peasenhall), W Catling (Sibton), R Blois snr. (Yoxford), H Johnson (Badingham), W Goodwin (Heveningham), Mrs Mann (Kelsale), Lord Huntingfield and Wells and Son of Saxmundham whose ironmonger's business still operates under that name today. A feature of the orders was the number of

8 SRO Ipswich HC23/F2/26

The Victorian Period

drills delivered to other agricultural implement manufacturers or other businesses such as Ransomes, Sims & Jefferies Ltd. (Ipswich), Barford & Perkins (Peterborough), Blackstone & Co. Ltd. (Stamford), I F Howard (Bedford), and Woods & Co. (Stowmarket) to name but some. On the continent drills went to C Duchamps (Brussels), E L Meyer (Hildesheim, Germany), Peterson & Co. (Copenhagen), Parsons, Graepel & Sturgess (Madrid), Antonio Sarmento (Lisbon), G Sundhoim (Spain), and Massee & Zoon (Goes, Holland) who received a large quantity. The meticulous records included the names of the craftsmen who had made the various parts of the drill, for example April 4th 1890 No. 19338 :-

Box   – Gardiner W
Frame   – Denny J
Levers   – Spall E
Wheels   – Davey D
Steerage – Jerry G

This particular drill was one of many ordered by Messrs Massee & Zoon of Goes, Holland and was consigned to Messrs Braakman & Co. Rotterdam.

9 Blacksmiths shop at Peasenhall Works. SRO Ipswich HC23/E1/1

The 19th century closed with the company firmly established as one of the leading British makers of agricultural drills with a high reputation and a steady flow of orders but any optimism for the future shared by owners and workforce was to be shattered by a number of catastrophic events that were to occur during the first quarter of the next century.

Chapter 3

The 20th Century

Great Britain's relative decline from a position of supremacy probably started around the turn of the century and by the 1960's if not earlier she had been overtaken by the United States of America, Japan and Germany as an industrial and economic power. Strangely, but co-incidentally, the decline of Smyth's follows a similar time-scale. There are other similarities insomuch as, while it may be fanciful to suggest that Britain's diminished power and influence originated with the death in 1901 of Queen Victoria, the death in 1908 of JJS was the first of several calamities that befell the company and set it on a downward spiral that would culminate in its demise in the 1960's.

It is true to say, however, that the company was already experiencing difficulties before the death of JJS. The continental trade, particularly France and Holland, was vital to Smyth's profitability and for many years they employed a general manager based at their Paris depot (previously in Dieppe) who co-ordinated the supply and distribution of drills.

In January 1894 JJS visited Paris where he met a Monsieur Gontier and appointed him as the Paris manager to replace M. Maraval on a salary of 4000 francs a year and one per cent of the cash received for business transacted in France. Details of this were included in a **9** letter of 3 January 1894 from JJS addressed *"Dear Mac"* (clearly this was Ralph Alexander Mac Smyth) and signed off *"Your affectionate Brother Josiah"*.

Moving into the early years of the 20th century it is evident from a letter sent by JJS to his sister Madeline that he was very concerned with the state of the French trade and important decisions had to be taken.

Dear Madeline,   *"March 24th 1906*

I enclose Notice of General Meeting which I hope you will be able to attend as I intend to hold a Directors meeting just previously and if Herbert can make it convenient to accompany you we shall be pleased to see him.

This meeting is really an important one as I want to talk over Paris matters. The lease that is expiring was for three 5 year terms and 15 years in all and (as things are going) it is fortunate for us, that it has only another year to run from now because it has ceased to be profitable and prospects are not improving and instead of being a "Feeder" to this business is becoming to be a "Sucker".

Matters generally on the Continent are looking anything but healthy. There are so many French makers now, that are copying our Drills and we are handicapped 10 per cent in the matter of carriage & duty, besides that French labour is cheaper, workmen work longer hours & the makers have no Paris expenses.

9 *SRO Ipswich HC23/C1/5*

French agents also and not unnaturally, lean to home makers as they can also allow larger discounts and their prices are lower than ours. In fact farmers there also begin to think that they are paying to much for our reputation especially the small farmers and the younger generations.

The "<u>South African War</u>*", indirectly hastened matters but English makers of Agricultural Implements (except Self-Binders) have long since had to give up the French trade pretty much.*

With kind love to all and trusting Aimee still keeps mending.

Your affectionate Brother,
Josiah

P.S. The only alternative would be to try and hire from year to year provided the proprietor of the Warehouse would consent and we see our way to doing so."

This letter was followed by a spate of correspondence between JJS and M. Gontier (Smyth's Paris Manager) which reveal the action taken with the intention of improving the deteriorating situation in France and in which M. Gontier played a central role; his **9** first letter was as follows:-

"Paris   March 30th 1906
Messrs James Smyth & Sons Ld
Peasenhall

Gentlemen

Yours of the 28th inst to hand and note contents of same.

Also your letter of the 29th inst enclosing notice for the proprietor of the warehouse. As soon as I received your letter I went to Ms. Iribout and asked to him whether he would be disposed to let on the warehouse from year to year, subject to six months notice to expire March 31st of any one year, and at the present rent.

He hesitated to reply me, but after all things considered, he replied me that he accepts your proposals to let on the warehouse from year to year. Consequently you will have to write to him in French the enclosed letter to which he will reply, so that it will not be necessary to have a new lease.

Yours very truly,
J Gontier"

This letter was soon followed by another:-

9

"Paris   April 17th 1906
Messrs James Smyth & Sons Ld
Peasenhall

Gentlemen

I went this morning to pay the rent of the warehouse, but could not see Ms. Iribout, as he was out of Paris, and it is why he desired an answer for last week.

I told to his clerk that you have decided to leave the warehouse at the end of the lease.

If you will no longer have a warehouse or depot in France, as you say, it will not

9 *SRO Ipswich HC23/C1/5*

be very easy for you to continue the sale of drills except in having a depository in an Agricultural implement house, as Pilter or other, as it is necessary to have an agency to supply the extra parts to the farmers who use your drills.

If I had the necessary money I should not hesitate to ask for the representation for France, and I should hire at once the actual warehouse as I am convinced that, in keeping it, it will be possible to sell drills for a long time; whilst in leaving out this warehouse, it will, I fear, do much wrong for the sales to come.

Yours very truly,
J Gontier"

Of course, M. Gontier had a vested interest in this matter as if Smyth's pulled out of France his position would be in jeopardy and naturally this would influence the advice he expressed.

M. Gontier wrote again on **9** 7 November 1906 saying *"I shall be glad to know what you are intending to do for the future"* and on 30th January 1907 when he said:-

9   "Paris January 30th 1907*

Dear Mr Smyth

The circulars, sent lately to inform agents of your intention to close Paris depot, were known rapidly by farmers, and they have made a very bad impression on account of the extra parts which it will not be possible to you to supply at once, the transport and custom formalities asking for 4 or 5 days even by grand vitesse.

Therefore I write again to ask for the general agency for France.

When Mr Rickards cames here, he told me that you intended to give me this general agency, and to grant me a commission of 20%, more 5% discount which, in granting 15%, more 2% to the agents, will permit me to have a profit of about 8% and sometimes 10% in the case of supplying farmers directly.

Hoping a favourable answer

I am yours very truly,

J Gontier"

The **9** circular sent by JJS to inform agents of Smyth's intention to close the Paris depot was brief and to the point:-

                                                  "8 Rue Philippe-de-Girard
                                                                Paris*

We beg to inform you that in consequence of suppressing our Paris House, Mr. Jules Gontier, who has been our Paris Manager for the last twelve years has been appointed our General Agent for France to whom all communications should be addressed after end of March next (1907).

9 SRO Ipswich HC23/C1/5

The 20th. Century

10 A Smyth seed drill made by craftsmen. The photograph was taken in the yard of the Peasenhall Works with the company offices and foundry chimney in the background. SRO Ipswich HC23/E6/7

In consequence of having to vacate Warehouse we cannot accept any more orders for Drills this season and future prices must be further advanced."

M. Gontier's requests to be appointed Smyth's General Agent for France had been granted and he wrote to confirm the terms of the appointment:-

9 "*Paris February 20th 1907
Messrs James Smyth & Sons Ld
Peasenhall*

Gentlemen

Replying to your letter of the 15th inst. respecting the Agency in France, subject to my written acceptance you are willing to concede to me the General Agency for the Sale of your Drills and Reserve parts in France & subject to your power of cancelling Same by giving six months notice, terminable July 1st of any year; and as regards drills, Should I not be able to find sufficient Capital, you to be allowed to supply to other parties, by allowing me 5% commission on such transactions if you wish.

Me on my part to engage to supply wearing parts to any person, against cash, with a reasonable profit.

The Agency also to cease in event of me failing to meet my engagements.

You to deliver free to South Eastern or London Brighton & South Coast Railway Company in London at English catalogue prices on not less than ten shillings worth of goods.

From London, me to pay the carriage and Duty.

The English prices of Drills to be subject to 22 1/2 per cent commission & 2 1/2 per cent discount for cash in one month from date of invoice. etc. etc.

You to allow me a limited credit of Three Hundred pounds English Sterling.
Yours very truly,
J Gontier."

No doubt M. Gontier was delighted to have secured the general agency but it seems his optimism for the future of business in France was not shared by JJS and about a year later he wrote a very cautionary letter:-

9 "*James Smyth & Sons, Ltd.,
Patent Corn, Seed, Manure Drill
Manufacturers, Ironfounders, etc.,
Peasenhall, Suffolk, England.*

Dear Mr. Gontier, *January 10th 1908.*

Yours of the 6th inst came duly to hand. As regards trade it remains to be seen how the present year works out; last years Balance Sheet works out satisfactorily.

9 SRO Ipswich HC23/C1/5

This years transactions with the Implement Agents will be the test because of the small profits that they are making, and we have to be very cautious that we do not make bad debts.

Bad debts are what we have to beware of.

I shall of course try my best to keep on another year in order to show another fair Balance Sheet.

My aim has been to help you what I can.
Remain yours sincerely,
James Josiah Smyth."

There is evidence to support the belief that Smyth's finally vacated their Paris warehouse in 1907 although M. Gontier continued to operate as their General Agent for many more years. Despite reducing the costs of maintaining a presence in France, it is apparent that only small profits were being made and JJS was very anxious not to incur bad debts.

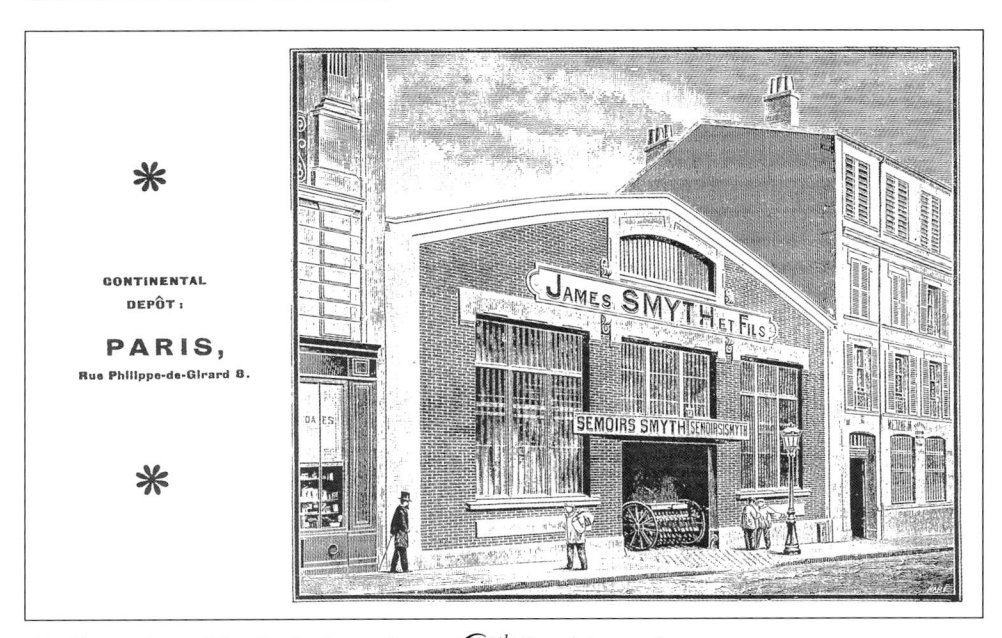

11 Illustration of the Paris depot from a 20th Smyth's catalogue.
SRO Ipswich HC23/E3/1

There is little doubt that during the early years of the 20th century the French trade was depressed causing serious concern at Peasenhall but this problem paled into insignificance with the death of James Josiah Smyth on 26th July 1908 at the age of 75 years.

The death of JJS was a hammer blow to the company because, despite his advanced years, he was vital to the well-being of its operations having grown up with the firm from boyhood and knowing the business in every detail as well as having an extensive knowledge of the industry and his competitors acquired during a lifetime's experience. The significance of his death and its impact on the business are due to the fact that, unlike his father (James Smyth jnr.) who had a large family and who had prepared James Josiah and his brother Herbert Ambrose to take over the business, JJS had no off-spring to carry on the Smyth dynasty and his brothers Herbert Ambrose and Ralph Alexander Mac, who had both been very heavily involved in the business, had pre-deceased him leaving the company without an established leader.

The ownership of the company's shares at the time of James Josiah Smyth's death is not known; the *10* last will and testament of Ralph Alexander Mac Smyth, who died in 1897 and was a major shareholder (he was described in his will as a managing director of James Smyth and Sons Limited), contained instructions to sell and dispose of his shares within a specified period and subject to certain conditions but who acquired them is not known.

· Similarly, the *11* last will and testament of James Josiah Smyth included instructions regarding his shareholding in the company viz; *"......but as to my shares in James Smyth and Sons Limited I direct that the same shall all be sold at the same time so that while my Trustees shall retain any interest in the business of the said James Smyth and Sons Limited they shall have control of the same business and I direct that all the said shares shall be absolutely sold and disposed of within two years after my decease...... "*

The trustees appointed in the will were the Reverend James Robinson Garrett of Helmingham Rectory, near Ipswich, Suffolk Clerk in Holy Orders, Albert Blackford of Chippenham, Wiltshire ironmonger and William Chandler Block of Ipswich solicitor.

12 A letter of 30th December 1908 (only a few months after the death of JJS) from Block and Cullingham, solicitors of Ipswich to Mr J S Rickards (company secretary to James Smyth and Sons Ltd.) shows that of the shares held by JJS 10 shares each were transferred to Albert Blackford (nephew of JJS), J H Blackford, Mrs L L Thirtle and Miss E C Blackford. Although no further evidence has been found, it is almost certain that the majority of the company's shares were held by people who were related to JJS by marriage, in particular members of the Thirtle and Blackford families who were to play a major role in the future and the fortunes of the company.

Two men who were employed at "the Works" for many years, Herbert Denny and Fred Rowe, were interviewed around 1990 by Mr Tony Martin, who farmed locally and who had a keen interest in Smyth drills, and they both said that after

---

10 SRO Ipswich   11 SRO Ipswich   12 SRO Ipswich HC23/A2/1

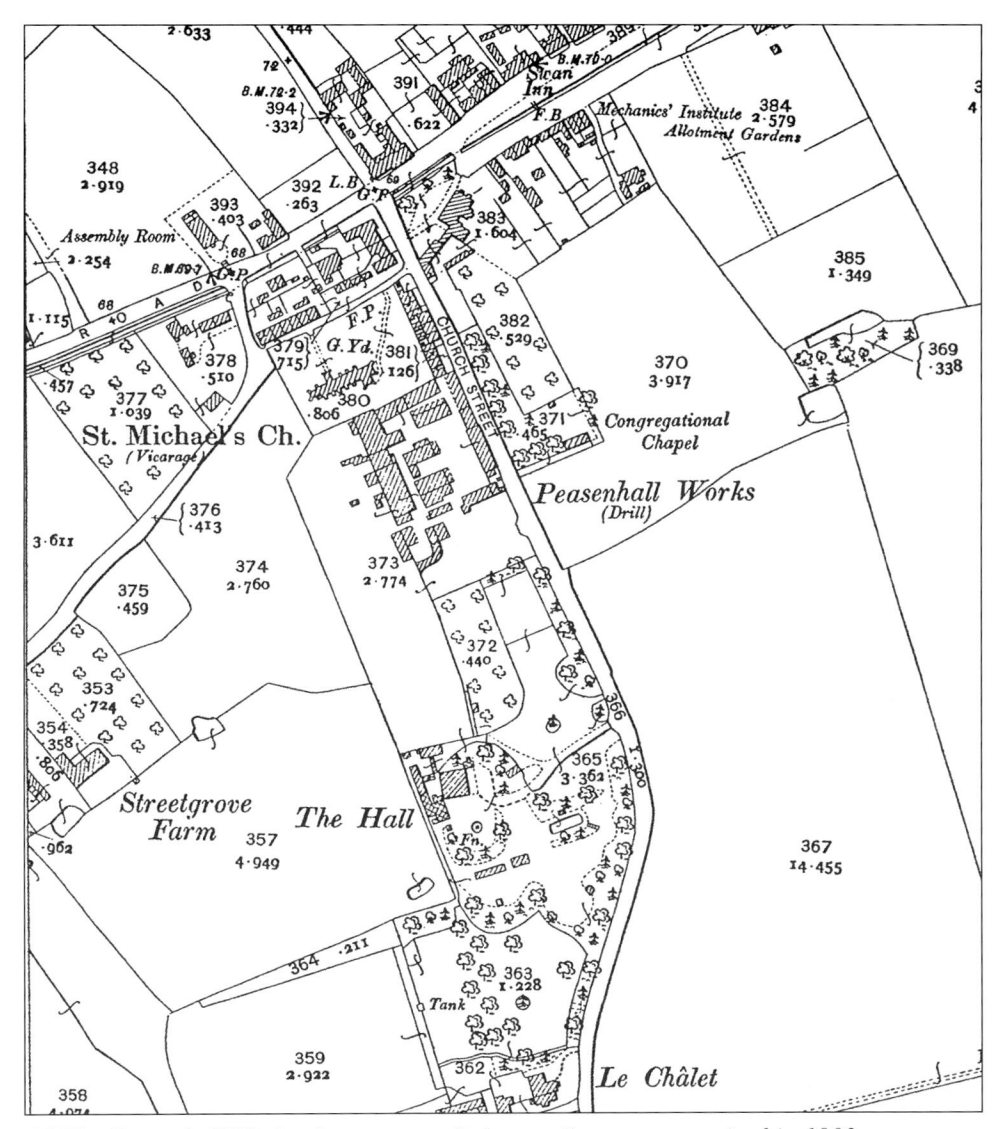

12 The Peasenhall Works shown on an Ordnance Survey map revised in 1903. The Hall, Le Chalet, Assembly Room and Mechanics' Institute are also depicted.
Ordnance Survey Office

JJS died the business was run by J S Rickards and he was followed by a Blackford and then a Thirtle. A letter on Smyth headed paper dated October 13th 1915 sent to Lance Corpl. F Burgess (an employee of the company) who was serving with the Suffolk Regiment in France during the First World War was signed by James Smyth Blackford and the text of the letter makes it clear that he was signing as "the boss". James Smyth Blackford died on the 27 December 1918 and he was succeeded as managing director by Thomas Henry Thirtle.

Herbert Denny remarked during his recorded interview *"After him (referring to J S Rickards) Blackwood (sic) took it over. Blackwood (sic) took it on, he was one of the family and he lived at The Chalet and after he died Mr Thirtle took it on. He came from Lowestoft and his wife was the biggest shareholder in the firm. She was one of the Smyth's and he carried it on for some time."*

Thomas Henry Thirtle lived at "Fernside", Yarmouth Road, Lowestoft and was a well known figure in that town; his father, Thomas Elvin Thirtle, was mayor of Lowestoft 1910-1912 (two terms) and in Kelly's *Directory of Lowestoft* 1909 he is described as an ironmonger of 45 & 47 High Street; blacksmith, Old Market Plain and boat owner Whapload Road.

And so the responsibility for taking Smyth's forward rested on Thomas Henry Thirtle a man with a business background and of course the infra-structure, marketing networks and skilled workforce that had been built up over many years were still in place. It is doubtful if JJS's absence had an immediate impact but rather that it contributed to the gradual decline in the company's fortunes.

That Smyth's drills continued to perform well after the death of JJS is shown in a long letter from Southern Rhodesia extracts from which are reproduced below:-

13

"March 13. 1912
Hallingbury Farm
Hartley, S Rhodesia
South Africa

Messrs J Smyth & Sons
Peasenhall Suffolk England

Dear Sirs

You will no doubt be pleased to hear the Nonpareil Corn Drill, which was purchased from you for us last October by Mr H Sparrow of Bishops Stortford arrived here safely on Christmas morning.

Having worked a similar drill for nearly 20 years in the Transvaal we had no difficulty in unpacking and putting it together. The only breakage was the 22 wheel on the second motion which should have been taken off for shipment. Fortunately you sent a duplicate so there was no delay caused by the breakage. We had the drill working the following day and it worked quite satisfactorily.

We have since drilled with it the following seeds:-

Manna (a variety of millet), Mangold, Kaffir Corn, Munga (another variety of millet), Teff Grass (a very small seed no larger than Gun Powder), Swedes, Wheat, Oats, Barley, Rye, and Nepal Barley, sometimes called Barley Wheat.

We have also been quite successful in making the Machine drill artificial Manure & Super Phosphate - This it does quite well provided one man rides on the front part & occasionally stirs the Manure to keep it moving.

13 SRO Ipswich HC23/F9/1

It has done all this work to our complete satisfaction. We use either four or six Donkeys as our motive power as there are no horses in this country for farm work.

Several of our neighbouring farmers and other friends have been to see it & are much pleased with it and the work it can do.

Mr. Godfrey Munday F.L.S. the Government Agriculturist & Botanist paid us a special visit to see the Machine & said he intended to order a similar one for the Rhodesian Government, & last week we had Mr. Eyles our local M.L.A. (or M.P. as you would say in England) who is also a very large Farmer, he also took full particulars of the Machine & expressed his intention of giving you an order. No doubt several other Farmers may do the same so we hope you will see your way to allow a commission on all orders you get from Rhodesia as we have been the sole means of introducing your Drill into this Colony, ours being the first machine of its kind in the Country, & there is likely to be a considerable enquiry for Drills in the near future."

The letter, which was signed *"Sworder Bros."*, goes on to compare the Smyth's Drills to the American drills, which *"are practically the only ones used in the provinces of the Union of South Africa",* making points for and against but it is not known if Sworder Bros. received any commission!

Further evidence of the high reputation of the implements made at "the Works" during the early years of the 20th century and the diversity of their customers can be seen in **14** *"Steerage book nos. 5809 - 9851"* which covers the period 29 August 1900 to May 1914; the book contains details of order book numbers, steerage numbers, number of rows, and names and addresses of customers against steerage numbers 5809 - 8692 but after September 1910 the names and addresses of customers were not recorded. Some of the prestigious or exceptional customers include:-

The Country Gentlemens Association, London

The Crown Agents for the Colonies, London S W

The Agricultural and Horticultural Association Ltd., London

The Western Counties Association, Bristol

The Duchess of Hamilton, Ledbury

The Honourable W Vanneck, Fressingfield

Baron Charles K S Dinsdale, Meesdon Manor

Avon Orchard Co., Evesham

Customers local to Peasenhall include:-

Mr. J J Creasey, Sibton

Mr. Creasey is described in White's Directory of Suffolk 1896 as farmer and farm steward to Commander E B B Levett-Scrivener, Abbey Farm

Mr T A Garrett, Peasenhall

14 SRO Ipswich HC23/F5/1

The 20th. Century

13 An aerial photograph of the extensive Peasenhall Works.

Mr Edward William Thain, Bramfield *Blacksmiths and Cycle Agents*

Edward Leigh Heseltine Esq., The Rookery, Yoxford

Charles William Ransome, Redwald House, Yoxford

Mr Henry Lovett, Brick Kiln Farm, Yoxford

Alfred Freeman, Laxfield *Carrier*

Mr Samuel Bolton, Dennington *Blacksmith*

Mr W M Aldous, Cookley *Farmer*

Mr F Hurren, Saxmundham

Arthur Thurlow, Valley Farm, Bramfield

Thomas Sheldrake & Son, The Thoroughfare, Halesworth *Harness Maker and farmer*

Grayston Bros., Heveningham *Smiths and Implement & Cycle Agents*

Mr James Berry, White House, Sibton *Farmer*

Steerages were also supplied to the following Suffolk engineers and agricultural implement manufacturers:-

Cornish and Lloyds Bury St. Edmunds, Page and Girling Melton, Woods and Co. Stowmarket, Ransome, Sims Ipswich, Dupont and Orttewell Sudbury, Field and Son Beccles, Elliott and Garrod Beccles.

The steerages numbers book also provides information on steerages that were supplied overseas:-

Messrs Massee & Zoon, Goes, Holland

Many steerages were supplied to this company.

Paris (for Spain)

Paris (for Ton Kin)

Paris (presumably to Smyth's warehouse; probably 50% of the steerages listed in the book went to Paris)

Messrs Sturgess & Foley, Madrid, Spain

Mr Ed Arlborn, Hildesheim, Germany

Messrs Jules Loraux-Fondu & Fils, Marbais, Belgium

G Duchamps, Brussels, Belgium

Mr F P Mockford, South Africa

M J Gontier, a Jumeauville, France (Smyth's General Agent)

From the above details contained in only one record book it is evident that the overseas trade continued to be a very important part of the business particularly in western Europe. This trade was soon to be severely disrupted if not almost destroyed when in the summer of 1914 the First World War erupted and parts of Belgium and northern France were torn apart by a bloody conflict that lasted for four horrific years.

The First World War which Britain entered in August 1914, and more especially its aftermath, was the second major event that would influence the future of the company. The turmoil on the mainland of Europe and the danger to shipping from the war at sea had an adverse effect on Smyth's overseas trade although surprisingly many drills and spares were supplied to both M. Jules Gontier in France and Messrs. Massee and Zoon in Holland until April 1917 when continental trade virtually ceased until after the war.

The home market held up reasonably well during the war despite a number of the work-force serving their country in the conflict including Albert William Hill who was killed in action on 30 September 1916; the details held by the Commonwealth War Graves Commission (C.W.G.C.) describe him as *"Age 37. Son of William Hill of Wortham, Diss, Norfolk; husband of Bertha Hill of 78 Cumberland St. Woodbridge, Suffolk. Employee of Peasenhall Drill Works."* Although not strictly a local man the fact that he was employed at "the Works" was sufficient for his name to be included on the Peasenhall war memorial.

Another casualty of the 1914-1918 War who is named on the Peasenhall war memorial is Arthur James Blackford who was killed in action on 17 January 1916, he was the son of Arthur Albert James Smyth Blackford and Adela Fanny Blackford of 4 Avondale Road, Gorleston, Great Yarmouth and evidently was related to the Peasenhall Blackfords.

Fighting between Britain and Germany ceased on 11 November 1918 but this did not lead to full order books and prosperity for Smyth's. No sooner had a degree of normality returned to international trade than the 1920s saw the onset of an economic and agricultural recession which was followed by the Great Depression of the 1930s.

15 The minutes of an ordinary general meeting of the company early in the 1920s tell their own story:-

"MARCH 2nd 1921

At the Twentyninth Ordinary General Meeting of JAMES SMYTH & SONS, LTD, PEASENHALL, held this 2nd day of March 1921 at the Works office, Peasenhall, the following Shareholders being present:-

Mr T H Thirtle (in the Chair)

Mr J H Blackford

Mrs L L Thirtle

Mrs A F Blackford

Mr F G Woodard (Secretary).

The Minutes of last years meeting were read and confirmed.

The Directors and Auditors' report having been laid and confirmed.

The Directors and Auditors' report having been laid before the meeting together

15 *SRO Ipswich HC23/A2/2*

with the detailed balance sheet and accounts of liabilities and assets of the Company which having made allowance for Depreciation and doubtful debts showed a net profit of £915.6.10 upon the transaction of the year 1920 to December 31st.

It was unanimously resolved that the Directors report be adopted and a dividend of 5 per cent be declared which will absorb £756.16.0 leaving a balance of £158.10.10 to be carried to the Reserve Fund.

Mrs Huson being the retiring director was unanimously re-elected.

It was agreed to recognise the services of William Cook (Foreman) being 73 years old by granting him an allowance of 7/6 per week and house rent free.

It was resolved to appoint a Working Foreman in his place.

It was agreed to reduce the price of drills a further ten per cent.

The manager was deputed to make enquiries as to the disposal of War Loan and Bonds.

Signed T H Thirtle, J H Blackford, E C Huson"

It is interesting to learn that William Cook was still working at the age of 73 years and his services were being recognised by granting him a weekly pension and rent free accommodation, the actions of a benevolent employer.

What is more significant, however, is the modest total amount being paid in dividends (£756.16.0 compared to £2557 in 1893) and a paltry £158.10.10 being carried to the Reserve Fund. This small return on capital and the decision to reduce the price of drills by a further ten per cent indicate the difficult trading conditions that were being experienced and that profitability was on a knife edge.

The names of the shareholders at the meeting confirms that ownership and control of the company rested with the Thirtles and the Blackfords and it was they who had to take important decisions concerning their investments in the business and the prospects for the employees whose livelihoods depended on the viability of the company.

As the company attempted to deal with the difficult trading conditions of the early 1920s, another disaster struck on Thursday, 30th. August 1923 when "the Works" was devastated by a fire which virtually engulfed the entire site. The fire was reported at length in the *16 East Anglian Daily Times:-*

"BIG BLAZE AT PEASENHALL

AGRICULTURAL IMPLEMENT WORKS GUTTED

CHURCH & COTTAGES IN PERIL

DAMAGE ESTIMATED AT OVER £10,000

A serious outbreak of fire occurred at Messrs James Smyth and Sons drill works at Peasenhall on Thursday afternoon, when almost the whole of the works

16 SRO Ipswich

The 20th. Century

14 The scene of devastation at the Peasenhall Works as a result of the 1923 fire.

15 This photograph illustrates the intensity of the 1923 fire.

were gutted. The fire appears to have started in the roof of the paint shop and carpenters' stores, and it is believed that it was occasioned by sparks from the foundry chimney, which ignited the timber in the roof, assisted by the strong wind blowing at the time.

Smoke was seen from this quarter about one o'clock, and the alarm was immediately given. A manual fire engine, kept at the works, was soon in action, under the direction of Mr S G Woodard, the firm's secretary, and every possible effort was made to extinguish the flames.

A strong wind quickly made the fire spread, and the task of the firefighters was soon seen to be a formidable one. Messengers were immediately sent for the Saxmundham and Halesworth Fire Brigades, and in the meantime the Peasenhall Brigade, assisted by many inhabitants and visitors of the village, did everything possible to keep down the flames. Fanned by the wind, the blaze grew, and spread from shop to shop in a very short time. The paint shop, the carpenters' shop, and adjoining assembling and fitting shops, and warehouses soon became involved. The Saxmundham Fire Brigade arrived about 2.30 p.m. Under the direction of Supt. Scopes, a strong effort was made to keep the fire from spreading to other buildings. A quarter of an hour later the Brigade from Halesworth, under Supt. W.T.Ward, were on the scene, and a good supply of water was directed towards the buildings. The sawshed and other smaller sheds were soon in flames, but here the fire was stayed, and the boiler room, blacksmith's shop, generating houses, and adjoining buildings were kept intact.

WOMEN TO THE RESCUE

The whole of the fitting shops adjoining the road sent out great shoots of sparks, and the road was for some time impassable owing to the heat. Trees and shrubs on the other side of the road were scorched. A row of cottages, close to the works, were in extreme danger, and only the work of the women saved these buildings. The women formed themselves into a chain, and buckets of water passed from hand to hand and the burning walls and timber near the cottages were extinguished. Many of the inhabitants had removed their furniture from the houses.

At one time it was feared that the village church, situated so close to the premises, would suffer, but fortunately it escaped. The united efforts of the brigades and other assistance kept the flames in hand, and before dark the fire was only in isolated spots in the gutted premises.

The damage is considerable, and it is feared will exceed £10,000. This is, however, covered by insurance. The consequences of the disaster are serious to the village of Peasenhall, as most of the men in the parish are employed at the works. The firm, which was established in 1800, are known all over the world for their make of Suffolk corn and seed drills. At this time of the year the firm were about to commence the work of manufacturing the drills, and other agricultural implements for the coming Spring. Fortunately the buildings saved include the *stores containing spare parts and completed orders, and it is hoped to continue to supply these."*

From the above report it is evident that the fire soon gained a hold and with inadequate fire fighting resources in the village, a time of delay of about 90 minutes or more for the fire brigades from Saxmundham and Halesworth to arrive at the fire, and the congested nature of the site, it was inevitable that massive damage would occur. The estimated figure of about £10,000 damage would be about £270,000 at today's value and, while it appears that the loss was covered by insurance, the fire was a huge blow to the company as it had destroyed most of their facilities and the ability to function effectively.

The management faced up to the catastrophe and set about rebuilding the site while operating temporarily from a saw-mill, carpenters shop, and blacksmiths shop which formed part of the estate workshops owned by Commander Egerton B B Levett-Scrivener R.N. the local Lord of the Manor; these buildings were located at the bottom of the drive to North Grange Farm on the Halesworth Road, Sibton and remain there today. The company's balance sheet for the year ending 31st December 1924 includes an entry

"Add Reconstruction

Labour	*£ 446 : 13 : 10*
Materials & Outside Labour	*£ 1784 : 9 : —*
Incidental Expenses	*£ 43 : 17 : 7*
	£ 2275 :— : 5" (£61,425)

and so once more the company were back at the Church Street site and ready to face the future.

17 A study of the company's accounts for the years 1924, 1927, 1928, 1930 and 1931 (these being the only known accounts available) shows that the future was bleak both for shareholders and workers; a dividend was paid to shareholders in only one of the five years (five per cent dividend in 1924); with the exception of 1924 when a small profit was made, a deficiency or loss was made each year which peaked at £1076 in 1931; "Works Wages" decreased progressively each year from £5374 in 1924 to £1422 in 1931 suggesting that the workforce had reduced, men were working part-time or hourly rates of pay had decreased.

Fred Rowe, when interviewed by Mr Martin, said *"They started to go behind after the First World War, then during the 1920s there was a slack period, then it was the same for a time during the 1930s. They came on again during the 1939 War because there was a demand for their drills."*

Reggie Friend, who was employed at "the Works" for many years and was also interviewed by Mr Tony Martin, said *"During the 1930s, this was during the depression, we worked a week on and a week off, during this time they also made wheelbarrows and tumbrills but they were too dear."*

17 SRO Ipswich HC23/B2/1

Employing as they did a high proportion of the working men of Peasenhall word of Smyth's problems spread to neighbouring villages and prompted an interest from Major F O Langley of Abbots Lodge, Sibton (Abbots Lodge is a substantial house that stands in extensive grounds near to St Peter's church) who wrote to Mr T H Thirtle on 29 April 1926:-

18   *"Abbots Lodge Sibton*

Dear Mr Thirtle,

I have had a word with Lord Huntingfield and it is quite clear that we may count on his active sympathy. Of course we cannot presume to interfere with affairs of the Company, but any interest which I may show on behalf of our Peasenhall fellows whose future is so intimately concerned, I am only too ready to extend and Lord Huntingfield will, I gather, assist. The fluctuations of the exchanges render continental trade probably impossible and certainly dangerous. Trade with the Dominions and the colonies is, however, a different matter. I have various connections and contacts, which might be of use; and Lord Huntingfield makes a a number of practical suggestions in which I might (with his invaluable aid) be of help to you in increasing sales in the imperial markets.

It is suggested, and I pass the suggestion on to you, that you should let me have precise facts and figures of your agencies & selling organisation in Canada, Australia, South Africa & New Zealand, so as to see where there is room for development.

Underlying Lord Huntingfield's suggestions is the general idea that I should put your organisation in touch with representatives of those countries who are in England, with a view both to "pushing" the sales of Smyth's drills and to seeing what other similar lines you could, with slight adjustments, make to supply other demands e.g. in the cotton-growing areas of the Empire.

What practical value all this may have remains to be seen. But there can be no harm in trying and we shall both be very glad if something can be done to develop your turn-over sufficiently to ensure the continued livelihood of our Peasenhall fellows.

Perhaps you will instruct your secretary to tabulate the information required and to let me have it? I shall treat it all, of course, of being in absolute confidence.
Yours truly,
F O Langley.
I return the balance sheet with thanks"

The letter was written on paper headed *"Brooks's, St. James's Street, S.W.1"* and Major Langley also used the address of 7 Fig Tree Court, Temple E.C.4.

Major Langley's attempts to improve trade by opening up new markets appears

18 SRO Ipswich HC23/A2/2

to have come to nothing and it can be seen from other correspondence that his interest to assist developed into an endeavour, with others, to take over the company. He aroused the interest of Sir Herbert Hambling of Rookery Park, Yoxford, Suffolk whose son wrote as follows:-

18   *"Rookery Park*
Yoxford
Suffolk

Dear Mr Thirtle,   *11th April 1927*

Mr Langley, who has been staying with us for one or two days, persuaded my Father to interest himself in your Company and he has arranged for an expert to go over your Works next Thursday the 14th inst. with a view to giving an opinion as to their value. His name is Mr Leggett.

Perhaps you will afford him the necessary facilities. The writer had the pleasure of going over your Works with Mr Langley last week with your Secretary, Mr Woodard.

Yours faithfully,
Guy Hambling
T H Thirtle Esq.
Messrs James Smyth & Sons Ltd.
Peasenhall. SUFFOLK"

Correspondence flowed between Major Langley and Mr T H Thirtle, and between Mr Thirtle and Mr J B Cullingham of Messrs Block and Cullingham (solicitors of Arcade Chambers, Ipswich) and various relatives who were shareholders; Mr Thirtle, in a *18* letter of 26 August 1927 to Miss K Blackford c/o Grimes Stores, Potter Heigham, Norfolk, said *"As explained to your Mother we were out to sell the whole business if at all possible, but businesses are difficult propositions to dispose of. It is not everybody who will come along to purchase especially as the present agricultural outlook is so depressing.*

Your Aunts and Uncle wish to leave in as little as possible, but, as the position is now it is a question of taking the best offer we can get, and therefore we require your consent to leave up to £1500 if necessary.

The prospective buyers suggested even a higher figure than this should be left in. Personally I do not see very great hopes now of anything taking place."

Another letter from Mr Thirtle around the same time summarises the position with great clarity:-

18 SRO Ipswich HC23/A2/2

The 20th. Century

18 22nd August 1927

Mrs S H James
16, Prome Court
Rangoon
Burma

Dear Adela,

Negotiations have been taking place with regard to the sale of the shares in James Smyth & Sons Ltd.

For the last 3 years no dividend has been paid on the shares and there seems no prospect of any improvement in the near future. Farming is still in a very bad way and Farmers are not in a position to buy our Drills. There is hardly any export trade being done.

It might be necessary before long to close the works and sell the property, in which case there would be very serious loss.

Major Langley who lives nearby is anxious to keep the works going so that employment may be found for the men. The following terms have been discussed:-

The shares in the Company which are of the nominal value of £15,136 to be sold for £14,000.

The Shareholders would receive £7,000 or £8,000 in cash and the balance in 6% Preference Shares in the Company. Another business at Melton might be amalgamated with ours and the two worked together.

The cash received for the shares would be invested and your Mother would receive the income. If the business were successful the Dividend on the Preference Shares would be paid and your Mother would benefit.

The Trustees have no power to carry out such an arrangement without the consent of all the children.

If the others agree to some such scheme will you consent thereto?

Major Langley, Sir Herbert Hambling and his Son would be Directors of the Company.

It is proposed to develop the business on different lines with a view to increasing output and providing more work.

The other Shareholders all agree and this letter is compiled by Mr Cullingham and myself.

Mr Cullingham suggest you should cable (deferred rate) your reply.

With fondest love.
Yours sincerely,"

The letter paints a bleak picture of the business in very serious difficulties; a dividend on the company's shares had not been paid for the last three years with little prospect of a dividend in the near future; farming was in a very bad way so

18 SRO Ipswich HC23/A2/2

farmers were not buying their drills and hardly any export trade was being done; the closure of the works was a possibility and this would result in a very serious financial loss to the shareholders.

"Another business at Melton" referred to in the letter was Page & Girling of Melton near Woodbridge, Suffolk who were described as *"Manufacturers of Agricultural implements, prize waggons and carts and iron and brass founders, heating engineers, general engineering repairs. Suppliers of everything for the estate, farm or garden."* Their plight was similar or worse than Smyth's and in 1930 they went into liquidation.

Negotiations between Mr Thirtle and Major Langley continued culminating in a proposal that provoked a terse response from Mr Thirtle.

18

> "Major F O Langley   7th October 1927
> Abbots Lodge
> Sibton
>
> Dear Major Langley,
>
> *I acknowledge receipt of your letter with the new proposals, which we are rather surprised at.*
>
> *The shareholders are unable to accept.*
>
> *Should you desire a further discussion on this matter will you kindly make an appointment."*

Mr Thirtle was evidently not pleased with Major Langley's proposal, which could not be regarded as generous, and his frustration was clear in the letter, which brought the following reply:-

18   *"Abbots Lodge,*
                                                    Sibton

> Dear Mr Thirtle,   10 October 1927
>
> *I have to acknowledge your letter of 7 October and to express my regret that the negotiations should, after all our trouble as to them, have thus collapsed. The difficulty of obtaining any satisfactory price in cash would appear to be insuperable so long as you can show no past profit, recently, to those asked to put that cash up.*
>
> *As to further discussion, it clearly would serve no purpose with regard to these negotiations. But if any other plan later on presents itself, I should be very glad indeed to discuss it with you and I feel quite sure that I could arrange for Sir Herbert's participation in such discussion. He shares my interest in the fate of the villages, and would be always ready, I know, to advise you. Let me know when and if you would like such a talk.*
>
> *Yours sincerely,*
> *F O Langley."*

18 SRO Ipswich HC23/A2/2

Major Langley had given the impression that he and Sir Herbert Hambling were motivated by concern for the future employment of Smyth's workforce and it would be unfair to suggest that they were driven by the opportunity to acquire ailing businesses for long term financial gain, however, they were intent to strike a hard bargain and their plans came to nothing.

Other offers were made to buy into the company during the very difficult times of the 1920s and 1930s including an interest from a Mr Bingham of Maldon who wished to buy shares to the value of £1,000 but the offer of £24 for £43 shares together with other conditions he required, proved to be unattractive to the shareholders.

This was followed early in 1931 with an attempt by a client of S A Waller, who acted as Smyth's accountant, to purchase all the shares of the company so as to gain complete control but this was unacceptable to one or two shareholders. This prompted an offer from Waller himself who was in a privileged position as the firm's accountant of knowing every detail of the company's financial state and their trading difficulties; despite the gloomy situation, he evidently saw a future for the business as in a letter of 26 February 1931 to T H Thirtle he offered to put in £4,500 on condition that 180 shares were transferred to him at £12.15.8 per share on the understanding that Mrs Blackford and Thirtle were prepared to leave their shares in the concern and Thirtle's experience of the business would be retained. This offer was rejected but an improved offer from Mr Waller was outlined in a letter from T H Thirtle to one of the shareholders:-

18   *"18th March 1931*

Dear Bert,

Thanks for your letter. I did write you in March 1929 but the letter was returned; it was to tell you about a Mr Bingham, from Bentalls of Maldon, who wanted to join our business. I sent a letter to Aunt Edith, which is the same as was sent to you and is as the copy enclosed.

With regard to Mr Waller's offer, it is purely on his own initiative. I know Mr Cullingham has written saying your aunt will not accept – I cannot understand Stanley, he was always saying what they were losing in interest and, now Mr Waller has given him a definite offer, he ridicules £50 or £60 a year as nothing. Personally I think Mr Waller has made a good offer, I know, neither you nor I would think of putting £2300 into the concern in its present state.

I told Mr Waller last Saturday the decision and was surprised when he said he would increase it to the following:-

18 SRO Ipswich HC23/A2/2

Mrs Huson	92 shares @ £13:11:8		£1249 : 13 : 4
Exors.of Mr J H Blackford	78	" "	1059 : 10 : -
Mrs L L Thirtle	6	" "	81 : 10 : -
Miss K Blackford	4	" "	54 : 6 : 8
			£2245 : - : -

The last two (10 shares), so that Mr Waller has the controlling interest. I saw Mr Cullingham on Monday and he is writing to Aunt Edith & Stanley with the new offer, and then on receipt of their reply, if favourable, he will let you know. Don't hope too much, I'm afraid they will stick out for a higher figure, which they will not get until something is done for the farmer.

Mr Waller would not make any offer unless I was leaving your Aunt's money in and I would keep with him, then he would put his ideas into the business.

Of course I know it is vital to your Mother, your other Aunts can live without it; I do hope for your sake the Snaresbrook people will re-consider it.

I know it is a sacrifice but no one can be blamed for the slump. You will see by the last balance sheet that every thing has been cut down to the lowest.

Stanley wants to make up all the stock and then close down - he does not know the difficulty. If we were to make up another 40 drills, with the iron and wages required, £1000 must be found and then you must find customers; meanwhile all other work must be refused and the trade would soon be taken up by another Firm. It is a problem and I am getting tired of the whole thing.

If I could get the £1250 now offered to Aunt Edith I should be satisfied but, as I said before, of course Mr Waller would not have this.

With love to you all,
Yours affectionately,

P.S. I have just heard from Mr Cullingham that your Aunt Edith has turned down the new proposal. I am sorry especially after the manner they have been adopting with regard to loss of interest. I am afraid Stanley thinks there is something behind the offer with Mr Waller and myself, which is certainly not so."

The letter is further evidence of the parlous state of agriculture and of Smyth's business where £13.11.8 was being offered for shares which earlier in the century had a nominal value of £43 each and yet Mr Thirtle considered this to be a good offer. A measure of mistrust between Mr Thirtle and other shareholders is evident as is the frustration he was suffering and clearly he would have preferred to rid himself of the unenviable job of running the business during a very difficult period with little prospect of improvement.

During the agricultural depression of the 1920s and 1930s it was increasingly important for Smyth's to promote their products in order to capture as much as possible of a limited market. Despite the costs involved, they exhibited at the

16 Photograph of James Smyth & Sons exhibits, Royal Agricultural Show, London (Park Royal). SRO Ipswich HC23/E1/1

Smithfield Show every year of the two decades with the exception of 1939 when the show was cancelled due to the outbreak that year of the Second World War. Some of the 1930s Smithfield Show catalogues reveal that Smyth's exhibited Scotch carts, pig feeders, chicken feeders, cattle pans and sack barrows as well as their stock-in-trade corn and seed drills. This suggests a belated and modest attempt to broaden the product range and diversify in order to widen the market for their products.

Smyth's also exhibited at the annual show of the Suffolk Agricultural Association which was *"Established 1831, for the Aid and Advancement of Agriculture, the Incitement of Skill, Industry and Good Conduct among Cottagers, Servants, and Labourers in Husbandry, and the Incitement of Enterprise and Emulation among the Owners and Occupiers of Land."* The annual show of the Association, otherwise known as the Suffolk Show, was held in 1928 at Bury St Edmunds where it attracted 130 exhibitors who were by no means confined to Suffolk as firms from as distant as Liverpool and Barnstaple in Devon were represented at the show. By way of example, the presence of the Chilean Nitrate Committee, the Southern Rhodesia Office of the High Commissioner, the Suffolk Sheep Society and the East Suffolk Federation of Women's Institutes illustrates

The 20th. Century

17 Smyth's stand at an agricultural show between the wars.

18 From left to right   Thomas Henry Thirtle, Fred Woodard, Herbert Paternoster and Charlie Howard at the Suffolk Show at Saxmundham during the 1930s.

the variety of the businesses and organisations represented at the show. Notable engineers and manufacturers of agricultural equipment and implements, other than Smyth's, included Clayton & Shuttleworth Ltd. Lincoln, Ruston & Hornsby Ltd. Lincoln and the local firms of Richard Garrett & Sons Ltd. of Leiston, Ransomes, Sims and Jeffries Ltd. Ipswich and Page & Girling, Melton, Woodbridge.

The benefits to Smyth's of exhibiting at various agricultural shows have not been measured but their regular attendances over many years suggests that there were advantages to be gained that outweighed the cost and time involved and, of course, this was a practice carried out by their competitors and had to be rivalled.

A feature of the 1920s and 1930s for Smyth's was that while many spares were ordered and supplied the number of drills ordered was far fewer than in earlier years. For example during a period of almost two years from 24 October 1927 to 9 September 1929 (*19* Order Book "H") the total number of drills ordered was 133 with many of these going to Messrs. Massee & Zoon in Holland and during 1931, although numerous spares were supplied, only 37 drills were sold reflecting the difficult trading conditions which were prevalent during these times.

Order Book "I" which covers the period 9 September 1929 - 24 November 1931 includes a number of orders from Wells and Son Ltd. ironmongers of Saxmundham for items such as fire grates and backs, furnace grates and doors, and heater stoves all made to order as replacements and, while these were minor orders, they would have helped with keeping the foundry supplied with work.

Another feature of the 20th century was the network of agents that Smyth's established throughout many parts of the country and a high proportion of drills and spares were supplied to implement makers and agents, agricultural engineers, iron founders, and ironmongers; examples of local agents who were very active include Grayston Bros. of Laxfield (formerly of Heveningham), Thain's of Bramfield and Bridges of Framlingham.

The last order from Jules Gontier, Smyth's long serving agent in France, was recorded on 26 February 1932 and an association which had lasted for almost forty years had come to an end together with Smyth's French trade.

Hire purchase was introduced in 1932 in an attempt to make it easier for farmers to acquire a drill and *20* Order Book "J" (26 November 1931 - 8 October 1934) contains the following entry:-

"Smyth's Drills (Hire Purchase Co.), Accommodation Agency, 4 Surrey Street, Lowestoft", however this initiative to boost trade was short-lived as only eleven drills were hired and the scheme was discontinued the same year.

Thomas Henry Thirtle had led Smyth's since 1919 bringing the firm through the economic and agricultural depression of the 1920s and 1930s with all the difficulties that created and his death in August 1938 would have been a blow to the company as for nearly twenty years he had brought consistency and business experience when it was badly needed.

19 SRO Ipswich HC23/F2/51   *20* SRO Ipswich HC23/F2/53

T H Thirtle was a Lowestoft man who was a well known personality in his home town and his death was well reported in the local newspaper:-

21   *"AUGUST 6 1938*
DEATH OF MR T THIRTLE
Town Councillor and Fire Brigade Chief

It is with great regret that the death is recorded of Councillor Thomas Henry Thirtle, Fernside, Yarmouth Road, on Monday. Mr Thirtle was the only surviving son of the late Mr Thomas Elven Thirtle, who was twice Mayor of Lowestoft _ in 1910-11 and 1911-12. He was also honorary chief officer of the Lowestoft Fire Brigade and to this post Mr T.H.Thirtle succeeded some years ago. He initiated various improvements, and brought the brigade to a high state of efficiency, which was always in evidence when fires occurred.

In May, 1934, there was a vacancy on the Town Council owing to the death of Mr.W.Bailey, and Mr Thirtle was elected. He was re-elected in November of the same year.

He took the keenest interest in St. Margaret's parochial affairs, and for some years was Rector's Warden. When he was re-appointed at the last Easter Vestry the Rector paid a tribute to his many good qualities and faithful service. Throughout the town he was highly esteemed, and there are many that will mourn him. He leaves a widow, two sons and three daughters, and to them the fullest sympathy is extended in their bereavement. He was 68 years of age.

The funeral is tomorrow (Saturday) at St. Margaret's, at 1.30."

21 The newspaper report of the funeral recorded that the coffin was borne on a fire engine and six firemen acted as bearers; the large concourse was representative of the civic, business, and social life of the town, and long before the time of the service the church was almost filled. Headed by Supt. Harper and followed by Supt. W. Mobbs, members of the Fire Brigade walked in front of the engine, a posse of the Lowestoft Police under Supt. H.E.Boreham following. Suspended in front of the coffin was the firemen's wreath with the initials "L.F.B." worked in red flowers.

Two dark stained oak kneeling desks were given to St. Margaret's church, Lowestoft by a number of friends of Thomas Henry Thirtle; they were designed by Mr. J N Comper, who was described in 1949 as *"the well known artist and architect, who has had immense experience in the furnishing of Churches and Cathedrals for the last fifty years,"* and are inscribed:- *"In Mem. Thomas Henry Thirtle Churchwarden 1922-1938."*

22 In the last will and testament of Thomas Henry Thirtle he is described as living at "Fernside", Yarmouth Road, Lowestoft in the County of Suffolk company director. He specifically bequeathed to his son, Frank Elven Thirtle, the

21 Lowestoft Journal   22 SRO Lowestoft

mayorial portrait of his father, Thomas Elven Thirtle, and the silver salver and silver ink-stand bequeathed to his father. "Fernside" was left in the trust of the trustees to permit his wife, Laura Louise Thirtle to use it during her lifetime and the contents of his house were left to his wife. His wife, Frank Elven Thirtle and his other son, Bernard Henry Thirtle were the trustees of the will which was granted on 1 December 1938.

"Fernside" is a substantial detached Victorian house which stands on the corner of Yarmouth Road and Park Road, Lowestoft.

The will contains no reference to James Smyth & Sons Ltd. or to shares in the company although there is no doubt he had been a major shareholder and it is probable that he had transferred his shareholding to his two sons before he died.

T H Thirtle had continued to live in Lowestoft while he was the head of Smyth's and it is known that during the latter years, if not before, he came to "the Works" only on a Friday and, for some time prior to his death, the day-to-day running of the business was left to his son, Frank Elven Thirtle, who lived at "Apple Tree Cottage", Middleton, Suffolk and travelled the short distance to Peasenhall each working day.

Frank Thirtle was described as managing director in a number of the essays produced by the Peasenhall school-children following their visit to "the Works" in 1950 and there is little doubt that in 1938 he succeeded his father as the head of the business. However, almost before he had time to take stock, in September 1939 the second major conflict of the 20th century burst upon the world and for more than five years normal trading conditions were totally disrupted. For Smyth's the experience of the Second World War, when compared to the 1914-1918 War, was different in two particular respects; firstly, a number of local women were employed to replace men who were in the armed forces and, secondly, the war brought a strong demand for agricultural drills as the country strove to increase food production and become self-sufficient.

Part of the German strategy to defeat Britain was to starve its people into submission by preventing the supply of imported food which was met by a determination, driven by necessity, to improve our own production of food and this created a demand for agricultural machinery and implements from which Smyth's benefited. The big surge in orders reached a peak in the period 5 September 1941 - 4 February 1943 when a total of almost 400 drills were ordered followed by 275 drills in the following period 5 February 1943 - 8 September 1944 as the war-time demand was boosted by substantial orders from the Ministry of Agriculture and the Ministry of Supply. The high level of production during the 1939-1945 was a tremendous achievement by the work-force denuded, as it was, of some of its skilled workers.

The 20th. Century

19 A gathering of the Peasenhall workforce to celebrate the wedding of Frank Thirtle 15 July 1935.
The individuals have been identified as follows:- Left to right. **Top row**. *Forest Bolton, Will Howard, Len Davis, Charlie Howard, Eric Howard (boy,) Bert Gardiner, Tom Gardiner; Stanley Paternoster; Herbert Paternoster; Sid Woodhouse,*
2nd row. *Reg Friend, Frank Howard(boy), Ted Friend, Lenny Rowe, Henry Nichols, John Denny, J Denny, Charlie Crickner, unidentified, J Rowe, Fred Self, John Whiting,*
3rd row. *Alfred Salter; Edgar Rowe, Jack Howes, Harold Howard, Walter Nichols, unidentified, Fred Gardiner, Fred Burgess,*
Bottom row. *Albert Rowe, Tich Kemp, Fred Woodard, (company secretary), Fred Rowe (clerk), William Paternoster, Herbert Chapman.*

The 20th. Century

20 The Peasenhall workforce enjoy a bottle of beer to celebrate Frank Thirtle's wedding on 15 July 1935.

Flight Sergeant Richard William Stiff was the only employee of Smyth's to lose his life in the Second World War; serving in the Royal Air Force he was killed on 13 November 1943, he is commemorated on the Runnymede Memorial, Surrey and on the Peasenhall war memorial.

Trade remained reasonably good during the immediate post-war years despite a huge reduction in orders from Holland which, managed by the agents Massee and Zoon of Goes, had been a corner-stone of the business during the 1920s and 1930s but this trade was never to be regained as technological developments started to impact on agricultural machinery and implements and Smyth's were left in their wake.

One of the reasons for the decline of Smyth's is said to be that their drills were made too well and therefore did not require to be replaced; the following letter provides evidence of the longevity, performance and versatility of a typical Smyth's drill:-

"6.4.57 (1957)   *Lorkins Farm*
                                                                                                  Orsett
                                                                                                  Grays
Dear Sir,   *Essex*

The photograph enclosed is of a Smyth drill purchased by my Great Grandfather in the year 1864. Bought second hand from a contractor who travelled from farm to farm. The drill has been in regular work every year since. Up to 1900 it drilled

53

well over a 100 acres a year, and since about 50 acres a year until this last war. Now it has gone up to 100 acres a year again.

The last time she drilled the field on the photo was 1896 when it was sown down to grass. It has been a meadow ever since until we ploughed it up this year and drilled with wheat with the same drill.

The drill is the original except for the coulters which we purchased from you during the last war. The number is 6336 Witham Essex.

My father and I are on the photo and he remembers having as many as six horses on it in the wet seasons.

Trusting this letter will be of some interest to you.
Yours faithfully,
J Wordley
for G. E. Wordley & Son
PS. My family has been in this farm since 1833. J. W."

This drill had been built to last by being hand-made by skilled craftsmen using best quality materials and it had given valuable service for the best part of a hundred years when the letter was written. John Wordley, the writer of the letter, still farms at Lorkins Farm and he has confirmed the drill remains on the farm and in good condition with the original wheels. The drill had been drawn by tractor from about 1941 until 1970, when it was last used, with no problems experienced although it needed two people to operate it effectively.

The business had experienced several recessions during its long existence and, with the exception of the duration of the 1939-1945 war when abnormal circumstances had stimulated demands for their products, successive managements had become used to operating under unfavourable trading conditions but during the 1950s they entered a downward spiral from which there would be no escape.

For one hundred and fifty years Smyth's had produced drills that were designed to be drawn by horses which in the early 1950s were being increasingly replaced with tractors and serious efforts were made to modify the drill to meet the demands of the market. Smyth's entry in the 1950 Smithfield Show and Agricultural Machinery Exhibition catalogue includes reference to a *"'Strong Nonpareil' 14-row, 8ft Wheel Track Corn and Seed Drill with Press Irons, Tractor Hitch, Rear Platform, and various small accessories"*; clearly an attempt to produce a drill that was suitable for use with tractors had been made. This was followed in the 1954 Smithfield Show with a *"'Strong Nonpareil' 12-row 8ft Wheel Track Grain and Fertiliser Drill with press irons, tractor hitch and various small accessories"* and a *"New-Medium Nonpareil 7ft. Wheel Track Corn and Seed Drill fitted with 4 rows; attachment for fertiliser placement, press irons, tractor hitch and rear platform."*

Notwithstanding the considerable efforts to produce and market a drill that was compatible with tractors and would also enable the simultaneous discharge of grain and fertiliser, trading success was not achieved. In 1962, following the death of Frank Thirtle in the previous year, the business was taken over by two local men, John Levett-Scrivener (the grandson of Commander Egerton B B Levett-Scrivener R.N. mentioned earlier) and Alec. Stearn.

The link with the Smyth's which had continued by marriage with the Blackfords and Thirtles had been broken after more than one hundred and fifty years and the plan was for money to be put into the business, which continued to trade as James Smyth and Sons Ltd., to design and make drills that were appropriate for the time, and for the business to develop.

There was no delay in producing a modern drill which was exhibited at the 1963 Royal Smithfield Show and was followed at the 1964 Show by *"The Smyth Multirow Model 22 Corn and Seed Drill"*; the drill was described as having a main frame consisting of rectangular hollow steel section, all steel wheels fitted with pneumatic tyres, and the following outstanding features:- *"1-man operation from tractor driving position; hydraulically operated; seed is controlled on and off automatically; cup feed mechanism; driving marker disks are automatically controlled; tractor wheel marks are eliminated by an automatic device fitted to the drawbar; folding drawbar for easy storage; coulters are spring loaded, tension easily adjustable."*

The launch of the Multirow Model 22 was accompanied with an eye-catching leaflet which proclaimed:-

IT'S THE NEW SMYTH CORN AND SEED DRILL

*Smyth drills have been world famous for over 160 years -
and rightly so. They are built by Suffolk craftsmen to
do a first-class job and to keep on doing it.*

*Now we have pleasure in introducing the <u>new</u> Smyth
22-row corn and seed drill that is bound to become an integral
part of today's power farming machinery.*

*It has many outstanding points. First and foremost, it is a one-man drill.
All the controls are simply worked from the tractor seat.
It is hydraulically operated. And it gives you <u>close spacing</u> -
although the drilling widths can easily be varied if required.*

*The seed box, with a large capacity, is fitted with a special
agitator which ensures an even flow of seed to the hoppers.*

*For a drill to meet the exacting demandsof twentieth-century farming,
there is nothing better than the Smyth <u>precision-built</u> drill.
It is built with a world of experience behind it.*

THE DRILL WITH A NAME BEHIND IT.

A new thirty two row drill (Model 32) was also introduced but unfortunately the new metal drill was not a success, the anticipated demand did not materialise and this led to the second change of ownership within three years when in 1965 the firm was bought by the Ross Group of Grimsby. The Peasenhall factory was managed by Johnson's Engineering Ltd., part of the Ross Agricultural Division, who marketed the drills under the name of Johnson-Smyth but the business was in terminal decline as between October 1962 and May 1968 only 25 drills were sold and on 30 April 1967 the production of agricultural drills in Peasenhall ceased, bringing to an end a way of life that had been followed by generations of local men.

23 Order Book (Sales) which spans the period 17 October - 14 May 1968 includes an entry *"Works Closed 30.4.67. Remaining entries delivered from Catchpole Eng. Co. Stanton 1967-8"*

The last order on the 14 May was for a Multirow 32 Drill to be delivered to Ernest Doe of Ulting, Maldon, Essex and the final chapter had closed.

What brought this once famous business to an end is open to speculation. The demise probably started with the death of James Josiah Smyth in 1908 as his passing deprived the company of a talented leader and without a successor with similar knowledge and skills; he had grown up with the business, he was a good engineer who had ensured that Smyth's led the development in drill technology, and he left a void that was almost impossible to fill. Those who followed him were not engineers, were lacking in knowledge of the agricultural business and, together with a dearth of investment in research and development, resulted in the products being left behind in markets that were changing and intensely more competitive with the advent of mass production.

The above analysis is not intended to be a criticism as, to the contrary, the continuous existence of the business for some one hundred and seventy years was a remarkable achievement by all those involved. As the business grew from a small wheelwright's shop to a factory employing a hundred or so people, the location would present transport difficulties as easy access could not be gained to the sea or the railways when they came. For long periods they operated in an unfavourable economic climate with the agricultural depressions of the 1880s and 1890s, and the 1920s and 1930s being especially difficult, and yet the business survived only to go the way of much of British industry in the second half of the 20th century.

Production may have ceased years ago but the legacy lives on and there is little doubt that in some remote place in Australia, or South America, or other part of the world, there stands an agricultural drill and on it are the words "SMYTH & SONS PEASENHALL SUFFOLK ENGLAND."

23 SRO Ipswich HC23/F2/67

Chapter 4
The Peasenhall Smyths

The Peasenhall Smyths lived in the village for more than one hundred years during which time their influence and effect on the local community was immense, the contribution they made to affairs of the village was of no less a scale, and evidence of their generosity, social responsibility, and position in the social structure of the time is to be seen in the built environment that they created or helped to shape.

James Smyth snr. was baptised on 8 November 1777 at Sweffling, Suffolk and he moved to Peasenhall towards the end of the century where he established his drill manufactory in 1800. He married firstly Elizabeth Roberson (died 1830) by whom a number of children were born and then Eleanor Williamson (died 1857); James Smyth snr. died on the 12 December 1843 aged 66 years and he, both of his wives and several of his children, Lydia (died 1832, aged 19 years), Phoebe (died 1833, aged 21 years) and George (died 1839, aged 25 years) are buried in St Michael's churchyard Peasenhall.

James Smyth jnr. (JS jnr.), the elder son of James Smyth snr., was baptised at Peasenhall on 15 March 1807 and married four times:-

His first wife was Sarah Gower who gave birth to Sarah Caroline (baptised 1832), James Josiah (baptised 1834) and Luisa Ann (died 28 April 1835 aged 14 weeks). She died in 1835 and is believed to be buried in Rendham Congregational church. He subsequently married Caroline who was the mother of Herbert Ambrose (baptised 1839 and believed to have died between 1864-1871) and Charles Augustus (baptised 1841) who had no connection with the drill works and is described in the 1861 census as a shopkeeper in Peasenhall. He next married Sarah Stammers (died 20 January 1847 aged 33 years) who is buried in St Michael's churchyard, Peasenhall. Mary Ann Jackson was the fourth wife by whom a number of children were born including Ralph Alexander Mac Smyth (baptised 1856, died 1897). She is commemorated on a stone obelisk that has a fine medallion portrait of her and the inscription:-

Sacred to the memory
of
MARY ANN SMYTH
Died
June 20th 1877
Aged 52 years

There shall be no night there

21 *The obelisk memorial to James Smyth jnr. and his wife Mary Ann in Peasenhall churchyard. A former Smyth's building forms the backdrop.*

James Smyth jnr. is also commemorated on the obelisk with the inscription:-

*Sacred to the memory
of
JAMES SMYTH
Died
December 8th 1891
Aged 84 years*

He that walketh upright walketh surely

Many successful Victorian entrepreneurs used their wealth to build imposing country houses which reflected their status in society and JS jnr. joined this trend when in 1846 he had built The Hall in Rendham Road just above the drill works. The Hall, although modest by comparison with some other houses of the same period, is an elegant residence in Regency style constructed of Suffolk white bricks and with fine cast iron balconies and brackets, reputed to have been made at "the Works", forming an attractive external feature. The house was set in extensive pleasure grounds and gardens and the whole estate demonstrated the owner's affluence and elevated position in the local social structure.

22 Peasenhall Hall built in 1846 by James Smyth jnr.

JS jnr. had built on the business he inherited from his father being described in the census of 1861 as *"Drill manufacturer and Farmer employing 65 men and 7 boys. Arable and Pasture land 38 acres"* and by 1871 this had changed to *"Corn Drill Manufacturer employing 104 men, 16 boys"*. The twenty years between 1855 and 1875 saw the peak of country-house building generated by agricultural prosperity together with new industrial wealth and that JS jnr. enlarged his workforce to cope with increased demands for his products points to him sharing in the prosperity that was being experienced.

The well-being enjoyed by wealthy landowners and industrialists was not shared by the majority of the population but the 19th century saw the emergence of a number of philanthropists, who were determined to improve the lot of their fellow men and families. Friendly or benefit societies were established as well as the provision of basic education for the children of less privileged parents. Municipal authorities provided libraries and technical institutes for the betterment of artisans and other working people, while in rural communities, reading rooms and similar facilities were often created privately by generous benefactors as a means for improving the education, knowledge and skills of local people.

Peasenhall was not left behind thanks to the public spiritedness of the Smyths and around the middle of the century they erected a building to house the Mechanics' Institute which was described in White's *History, Gazetteer and Directory of Suffolk 1891-2* as *"THE MECHANICS' INSTITUTION, established in 1855, has a library of 200 volumes, a good reading room, and about 60 members, who each pay a subscription of 6s. a year."* Not entirely free but no doubt good value for money!

The rules of the Mechanics' Institute are set out at Appendix A.

The solid looking, brick building that housed the former Mechanics' Institute and Reading Room stands on The Causeway next to the Old Thatched House and has been used as residential accommodation for some years.

A benefit society for Smyth's workers soon followed the formation of the Mechanics' Institute when in 1865 the Drill Manufactory Benefit Society was established; the rules were set out in a pamphlet printed by John Day, Quay Street, Halesworth, Suffolk and they are reproduced at Appendix B.

From the treasurer's account book for the period 1873 to 1896 it can be seen that the secretary was paid a yearly salary of ten shillings, ten shillings a year was also paid to the secretary of the Mechanics' Institute for the use of a room, and Doctor Lay, who presumably issued the doctor's notes that were required, was paid on average about £4 per year for his services. During the period a number of funeral allowance payments were made including one recorded on 16 March 1895 *"paid sick allowance and for coffin £1.14.0."*; on 23 December 1873 three months subscriptions were refunded to members amounting to a total of £7.6.0., and on 20 May 1874 steward John Ludbrook received one shilling for making a journey to Kelsale to visit a sick member.

23 The building formerly used as the Mechanics' Institute can be seen on the left of this old photograph of The Causeway, Peasenhall.

At a meeting of the Peasenhall Drill Manufactory Benefit Society held on 6 December 1876 at the Mechanics' Institute the society's rules were amended when it was unanimously agreed that the following should be added to the list of rules viz.

"If any of the Members did not pay the usual monthly subscription within a week after the day appointed to collect it, they shall be fined 6d. each; also that 1/- fine be imposed upon any Member who refuse to act as Stewards."

Undoubtedly the Smyth's benefit society fulfilled a valuable welfare service by providing financial assistance when a family's wage earner was unable to work due to sickness, or to meet funeral expenses.

The terrace of Victorian cottages in Church Street, Peasenhall (Numbers 1 to 7) were built by the Smyths to provide housing for some of their workers and they serve as a physical example of their enlightened attitude towards their workforce.

The more striking example of the family's benevolence and generosity is the village hall erected in 1888 by James Josiah Smyth for the use and benefit of the people of the village; the building, known during its earlier years as the Assembly Room, is constructed of wood in the style of a Swiss chalet reputedly to remind JJS of one of his favourite countries and its distinctive design makes it a feature of the village to the present day.

James Smyth jnr. in 1874 was elected the chairman of the Peasenhall School Board, which was established as a consequence of the Elementary Education Act of 1870, with JJS in the role of clerk to the board. The contract to build the new schools was placed with Messrs. Gibbs and Son to the design of the architect Mr

J Butterworth of Ipswich. The opening of the new school on 29 March 1875 was an historic day as it brought statutory education to the village for the first time and naturally the event was reported in the local press; one or two extracts from the press report make interesting reading:-

"Mr James Smyth, the chairman, having congratulated the meeting on the happy issue of the year's work of the School Board, first called on the Clerk (Mr Josiah Smyth) to report the history of the Board's labours, which that gentleman did in a very clear and business-like way, showing that from beginning to end - from the unavoidable resolution of the parish to elect a School Board, to the latest detail of the work - the greatest pains had been taken to secure efficient schools, and, at the same time, not needlessly to burden the ratepayers. The selection of an architect, the acceptance of the tender of Messrs. Gibbs and Son (the lowest), the borrowing of the money required from the Public Works Loan Commissioners, to be paid back (principal and interest) in 50 years by annual instalments of £4.5s.3d. per cent.; the passing of the Bye-laws, the appointment of the master and mistress (Mr H and Miss O'Donnell), and the careful selection of school fittings, were all related in a way that made it impossible not to see that the office of School Board was a most arduous one - at least for the first year, and that in this case it had fallen into the most able and capable hands."

24 Peasenhall village hall, formerly the Assembly Room, built by James Josiah Smyth for the benefit of the people of Peasenhall.

Mr W Crisp, a member of the school board, spoke about the benefits of education and the efforts of the board of which he said *"As to the efforts of the Board, he and his colleagues had used their position conscientiously - always acting "on the square" - and he had no fear that the ratepayers would be satisfied with what they had done. Before the meeting separated, he wished to move a vote of thanks to the Chairman.*

This having been carried by acclamation, Mr James Smyth responded. The Board, he said, not withstanding some adverse criticisms, had done their duty - not less and not more than they ought - and he trusted that while their labours were appreciated by the parish at large, the rising generation would reap a large harvest of good. He had been appointed chairman, he said, not for his ability, so much as that he was known to "act on the square", and perhaps his greatest service to the Board had been enlisting the services of his son as clerk, and he might quote the remark made by members of the Board as soon as that appointment was secured, "Now we shall get on!". He had special reason for interest in the education of that parish, inasmuch as the majority of the children were those of his own employees, and he was thankful that a sound elementary instruction on a religious basis had at last been provided.

Votes of thanks were then passed, first (with great enthusiasm) to Mr Josiah Smyth, the clerk, and then to the Board collectively, and after short replies from the Clerk and from Rev. W. Stock, on behalf of the Board, the meeting was closed with the National Anthem."

James Smyth jnr. and his son James Josiah had united to take leading roles on the School Board, they had displayed their willingness to play a major part in the affairs of the community and used their business expertise and drive for the benefit of local people.

Peasenhall's vicarage was built in 1873 on Mill Hill at a reported cost of £1473 (£59000) and was in the patronage of JJS. Kelly's 1875 *Directory of Cambridge, Norfolk and Suffolk* informs that:- *"The living is a vicarage, yearly value £140, with residence, in the gift of J.Josiah Smyth, esq., and held by the Rev. William Stock."*

Within a few years the financing of the living proved to be a problem and this resulted in the forming of the Peasenhall Living Augmentation Committee whose members included James Smyth jnr.. In October, 1880 the committee issued a printed circular letter part of which is reproduced below:-

"Sir,

Permit us to solicit your kind assistance in the cause we are pleading.

PEASENHALL was separated from the mother parish (Sibton) in the year 1871, and virtually became a new Parish, inasmuch as it had

NO PARSONAGE HOUSE - NO SCHOOLS -

AND A VERY POOR CLERICAL STIPEND (£135)

A Parsonage House and Schools have since been built, and it is now proposed to augment the living so as to make it more in keeping with the extent of population (about 1000).

Considering the difficulties with which the parishioners have had to contend from first to last, and in which they have not spared themselves, the Committee feel that they can consistently and fairly solicit the sympathy and help of all well wishers to the cause of true religion, and especially those who are placed in more fortunate circumstances.

The Patron has shown by his appointment and by his liberal help in the past, that he is actuated by no pecuniary motives, but has the highest interest of the parishioners at heart, and we feel in offering to contribute £500 to assist in creating an Augmentation Fund he has done as much as can be reasonably expected from him under the circumstances explained in his letter appended hereto.

It is hoped that by the united efforts of the patron, parishioners and others who may be willing to assist, this Fund may reach the sum of £1,500; and application has been made to the Ecclesiastical Commissioners for a Grant of a like amount."

The letter continued with a request for contributions to be paid to the treasurer before 31 December 1880, confirmed that the augmentation scheme had the support of the Bishop of the Diocese and of the Archdeacon of Suffolk, who had both kindly contributed to the fund, and ended with an assurance that contributions, however small, would be thankfully received by the treasurer or by any member of the Committee.

The letter was signed by Charles White, Treasurer and W.R.Bilney, Secretary.

The patron referred to in the above letter was of course JJS who issued the following printed letter:-

"COPY OF LETTER FROM PATRON

To the Committee of the Peasenhall Living Augmentation Fund

Dear Sirs,

In the matter of the augmentation I am wishing to do what I can.

In purchasing this Living I had, (as you know,) no family interest to serve, my only motive being that of securing a ministry acceptable to the Parishioners generally.

What with the purchase of the Living and my contribution to the Parsonage House Fund I have disbursed some £800 and now that I have presented to a young life the Living is of little pecuniary value. I am however willing to contribute £500 on condition that not less than that amount be raised by Voluntary Contributions, (or in other words up to £500 I subscribe £ for £).

I am, Yours truly, JAMES J. SMYTH."

A list of "Subscriptions already promised" was appended to the letter with the many subscribers ranging from the Honorable and Right Reverend Lord Bishop of Norwich (who subscribed £10) to "A Friend" (who also subscribed £10). The total amount promised at that point was £435.18s.6d. with the largest single donation of £100 coming from James Smyth jnr. Once more JJS had taken the lead and the initiative for the benefit of the parishioners and both he and his father had been generous with their financial support and involvement.

The beneficence of the Smyths in their support for the church in Peasenhall is also illustrated in a 1876 pamphlet details from which are reproduced below:-

"PEASENHALL
Parochial Collections, etc. 1875

The Vicar and Churchwardens have pleasure in submitting the following statement of the various sums contributed for Church purposes and other Charities during last year.

May 5th. 1876".

Society for the Propogation of the Gospel in Foreign Parts.

The total remitted to the Society was £5.19s.2d. which included five shillings each from Mrs H Smyth, Mrs James Smyth and Mrs Josiah Smyth.

"Organ Fund, for which further subscriptions will be thankfully received."

Miss Smyth had promised £10 and Mrs Smyth £5.

Coal and Clothing Clubs.

324 Bushels of Coal had been distributed at a cost of £16.4s.0d. and bills for clothing of £5.17s.0d. had been met.

Messrs. Smyth & Sons had donated 10 shillings while Mrs James Smyth and Mrs Josiah Smyth had each given five shillings.

Church Bells Restoration Fund, collected by Mr H Newson.

"Nobody's money, per J Smyth and Sons £11.8s.0d., Mr James Smyth £5.15s.0d. and Mr Josiah Smyth to make up deficiency 16s.11d."

Lighting Church Path (including Porch), collected by Mr H Newson.

Mr James Smyth gave £1.11s. 6d., Mr Josiah Smyth gave £1.1s.0d. while Mrs H Smyth donated five shillings.

Lighting Church with Lamps, collected by Mr H Newson.

Mr James Smyth gave seven shillings and sixpence. The Smyths were unstinting in their financial support for the church and JJS in particular played a leading role in the work of the church serving as he did as churchwarden for many years.

Not only were the Smyths committed to the affairs of the church, they were also involved in the running of the parish and both James Smyth jnr. and JJS held various responsible offices that were required for the functioning of what amounted to a parish council in Victorian times. What were known as vestry meetings were held for the purposes of appointing "officers" and setting rates which were set for expenses in relation to the county rate, police rate, union house (the workhouse), asylum, etc. The Vestry Minute Book 1850-1872 records that at a Vestry meeting held the 25th day of March 1851 Mr William White and Mr J Smyth were appointed assessors in respect of parish rates and at the same meeting Mr Thomas White and Mr J Smyth were nominated Guardians for the ensuing year. The Minute Book also contains the following record:-

"March 24th 1855

At a vestry meeting held this day when the following persons were present:-

Mr T White – Church warden

Mr J Smyth – Church warden

Mr Tunney, Mr Cole, Mr Moore, Mr Sampson, Mr W Robinson, Mr Baldry."

At this meeting Mr James Smyth was elected a foreman assessor for the ensuing year and it was recorded *"At this meeting Mr Lay the Parish Surgeon behaved in a most unbecoming manner to the Chairman Mr Thomas White the meeting afterwards adjoining to the Swan Inn for an hour.*

(Signed) Thomas White, Chairman

Mr Thomas White, Churchwarden

Mr J Smyth, Parish Warden for the ensuing year."

It is to be hoped that Mr Lay and Mr Thomas White settled their differences over a drink in the Swan Inn!

The latter part of the 19th century saw the creation of county, district and parish councils as central government introduced major changes to local government and the Smyths were very much involved in this process both locally in Peasenhall and further afield. In December 1894 Peasenhall elected its first parish councillors and this was followed by the first parish council meeting on 4 January 1895 when James Josiah Smyth was elected chairman and Mr C.E.Lay vice-chairman; JJS's brother Ralph Alexander Mac Smyth shared the family's sense of public duty by also serving as a councillor on the first Peasenhall parish council. The two brothers had horizons beyond their home village and from many copy letters contained in a letter book which covers the period April 1885 - December 1903 it is apparent that they were greatly involved in politics and played a leading role in the Yoxford District Liberal Association; JJS especially was very active in campaigning, organising meetings and supporting the Liberal cause and he went on to serve from 1889 to 1898 as an alderman on East Suffolk county council.

In a letter to a fellow Liberal JJS remarked *"Peasenhall is very Liberal I am happy to say also many parishes around"*, whether the working men of Peasenhall voted Liberal because the majority of them worked for JJS and were well aware of his political persuasion is open to speculation. However, there is no doubt that he was a supporter of the working man and his entitlement to be treated properly and fairly and this motivated his political ambitions.

Shortly before the sweeping changes to local government occurred James Smyth jnr.'s long life came to an end on 8 December 1891; his last wife, Mary Ann, had died in 1877 and in the 1891 census he was shown as living at The Hall, Peasenhall with his daughter Mary Ada Madeline, Emma Pearce nurse, Elizabeth Clarke cook and Maryann Thurlow housemaid. Not surprisingly for a man of his social position and eminence in the business world, a lengthy obituary was published in the main local newspaper, extracts from which are reproduced below:-

24 "EAST ANGLIAN DAILY TIMES, FRIDAY, DECEMBER 11, 1891.
DEATH OF MR JAMES SMYTH
OF PEASENHALL

A well-known figure in the manufacturing history of Suffolk, and indeed of England, has just passed away, quitting his hold on life so quietly at the venerable age of 84 years as to render the passage from this world to the next almost imperceptible to those around his death-bed - a fluttering as it were from one stage of being to another. Mr James Smyth, the octogenarian head of the important firm of James Smyth and Sons, of Peasenhall, Suffolk, and Witham, Essex, died on Tuesday at 9.50 p.m., at his residence at Peasenhall - it may be truly added, beloved and regretted by all who knew him.

The deceased gentleman's bodily health began to fail some two years since. He had for a longer period suffered from partial blindness, whilst latterly his mental faculties had given way under the accumulation of years, but his physical vitality gradually ebbed out with no apparent symptoms of bodily disease. His medical adviser, Dr Abdy Collins, of Saxmundham, was solicitous in his attendance on the good old man, the tidings of whose death - although, of course, far from unexpected - were received by his numerous body of employees and by his fellow-parishioners with a feeling akin to the actual death of personal bereavement.

The late Mr James Smyth was born at Peasenhall in the year 1807, and in 1836 took over from his father the business of manufacturing corn drills on the lever principle, which in the process of years has become of such vast moment in the agricultural production, not only of this kingdom, but of continental countries and the Colonies, and had continued to constitute an important industry in the village life of Peasenhall, whilst adding materially to the high reputation which Suffolk implements enjoy amongst the civilised nations of the world.

When in 1836 the gentleman now dead took over the business he indicated the same spirit of application to make it go-ahead which had been characteristic of his father. A branch establishment was opened at Witham in 1844, and another in France in 1860, and these today are virtually pregnant of business. In the early part of his business career Mr Smyth felt the importance of looking

24 SRO Ipswich

to foreign markets; and experiencing his own disadvantage as regards foreign languages, he had his sons educated on the continent, an expense for which he was in after years well repaid so that now all over Europe the name of the firm is well known. He was amongst the oldest exhibitors and members of the Royal Agricultural Society of England, having exhibited in 1840 at Cambridge - the second show held by that Society - and he had been a member since 1842.

He leaves behind him in the business two sons, Mr James Josiah Smyth, his eldest son, having been with him in it since 1849 and as partner since 1857. His youngest son, Mr R.A.M.Smyth, is also actively associated with the work of the firm, his services in representing which at the Royal, the Smithfield (where he is this week) and other great shows, as well as in a less public manner, have for a good many years been most valuable. The trade of the firm has continuously grown, and the annual output of drills is over 500, which are exported to all parts of the world, the principal trade being with France, Holland, Belgium, Germany, Spain, Portugal, and the Colonies.

The late Mr Smyth who was four times married, leaves three sons and five daughters. Throughout his life he was staunch in his adhesion to Liberal politics, and although a churchman, was no sectarian. In him the working classes of Peasenhall lose a well-tried generous friend, who was ever willing to help his needy neighbour, without the least inclination towards doing so in an ostentatious manner. He could not bear anything like oppression, and was ever a thoughtfully considerate employer, and a friend on whose trusty allegiance the utmost dependence could be placed. For some years he ably filled the office of Guardian of the poor of the parish of Peasenhall.

His son, Mr J.J.Smyth, who now becomes the head of the firm, was on the formation of the East Suffolk County Council in January, 1889, elected without opposition for the division of Walpole, and was chosen as an Alderman at the first meeting of the Council. Like his father, he is Liberal in politics.

The funeral is fixed for Monday next, at 3 p.m. in Peasenhall Churchyard, where the mortal remains of the deceased will repose in close proximity to the works which he did so much to extend in their local importance and international significance."

With the passing of James Smyth jnr. an important chapter in the story of the Peasenhall Smyths had closed and their future was in the hands of the third generation. He had built successfully on the business foundations laid by his father, extended "the Works" to provide the facilities to meet increased demand for their products, and saw the importance of overseas trade which he cultivated. He had gained a reputation as a good employer and shown generosity in his support for the church and other good causes that were for the benefit of many.

The family's responsibilities for the business and the community now rested entirely on the shoulders of JJS and his brother Ralph Alexander Mac Smyth. Although R.A.M.Smyth appears to have lived slightly in the shadow of his older brother, he undoubtedly played a major role in the company and held a senior position in the local social order. White's 1885 *Directory of Suffolk* gives his place of residence as "Sunnyside", Peasenhall, by 1888 he was living at "The Chalet" and the 1891 census confirms he was living at "The Chalet" with his wife Emily Jane and Mary Stannard who was described as a general servant (domestic). Following his father's death, this substantial detached house with numerous outbuildings on Rendham Road, Peasenhall in 1892 came into his ownership. The property is now known as "Bay House".

R.A.M.Smyth in 1894 presented to St. Michael's church Peasenhall a new organ but he had not long to enjoy its music as in 1897 his life came to an end at the early age of forty one years; affixed to the church organ is a metal plate inscribed:-

This organ was erected in 1894
The gift of Ralph Alexander Mac Smyth
In whose memory this plate
was affixed by the congregation
1897

10 In the last will and testament of R.A.M.Smyth he is described as *"a Managing Director of James Smyth and Sons Limited"* and his comparative affluence can be judged from the bequest to his wife Emily Jane:- *"........I give and bequeath to my said wife all my watches jewels ornaments of the person and wearing apparel and all my plate plated articles furniture linen glass china pictures prints musical instruments books and other articles of household use or ornament horses carriages saddlery harness and stable furniture brewing utensils live and dead stock tools implements and utensils and wines liquors and household stores and provisions and also all my cash in the house and cash at the Bank on current account and also all my crops of corn and other agricultural produce both growing and severed horses and other livestock implements of agriculture and other deadstock and effects for her own absolute use and benefit......"*. The will also contained instructions as to the disposal of his shares in James Smyth and Sons Limited.

From the list of his possessions the impression could be gained that R.A.M.Smyth enjoyed a good and pleasant life style and that being in the seed drill business had its benefits.

With the death of James Smyth jnr. and R.A.M.Smyth only James Josiah Smyth remained to carry on the family's work of running the business, providing employment for local men and acting as benefactors.

The 1891 census shows JJS, his wife Louisa Ann and Elizabeth Gilbert (general servant (domestic)) living at "Belle View" a house on Mill Road Peasenhall which was built for him in 1860. When constructed the imposing detached property, with its ornate front facade and multiple Tudor type chimneys,

10 SRO Ipswich

would have reflected JJS's wealth and social status. Internally the house is largely unaltered and features a fine, decorative central staircase as well as an unusual coat stand constructed of metal pipes which was connected to a hot water boiler in the cellar and designed to ensure that JJS could put on a warm coat before facing the cold of winter! Within the widespread grounds of the property there is a stable block built in the same Swiss chalet style as the village hall and this was used originally to house the carriage and horse that JJS used to get to and from the business.

The house has been known as "Millrise" for some time.

25 Belle View the Victorian home of James Josiah Smyth.

As the end of the 19th century approached every city, town and village in the country considered what to do to commemorate Queen Victoria's diamond jubilee in 1897. Peasenhall decided to mark the event by providing a clock for St Michael's church and the Rev. Ernest A Cooke contacted John Smith and Sons, clock makers of the Midland Steam Clock Works, Queen Street and Market Place, Derby whose letter paper claimed they were *"Makers of Clocks at S.Paul's Cathedral (The order being given on the recommendation of Lord Grimthorpe)."*

John Smith and Sons duly responded to the Rev. Cooke's enquiry with the following letter of estimates:-

Reverend Sir   *"January 30th 1897*

We beg to thank you for your much valued favour and in reply now do submit to you several alternative estimates for such a clock as would be suitable for your tower - the clock we propose would be of the very finest quality and workmanship and we should guarantee it to maintain perfect accurate time with less variation than <u>15 seconds a month</u>. We may inform that we made the new great clock for <u>St Pauls Cathedral</u>. The large clock for the <u>London School Board</u> offices and many other important ones.

Estimate l

We hereby offer to make and erect a clock in your church tower, to have no dial but to strike the hours upon the largest bell, to be fitted with all the latest improvements, to have apparatus to continue the action of the clock during winding, to have a small dial on the movement by which the clock would be regulated and adjusted.

<u>The main frame</u> *of the clock would be of one solid iron casting planed smooth and true with all the various wheels levers and other working parts arranged upon it in such a manner that any separate part might be removed without interfering with the remainder.*

<u>All the wheels</u> *would be made according to the recommendations of Lord Grimthorpe (the greatest authority on such clocks) the teeth being carefully shaped so as to work with perfect smoothness into each other.*

<u>All the arbors</u> *would be of the best cast steel properly hardened and tempered.*

<u>The pendulum</u> *would be a cylindrical one with heavy domed top bob - fitted with screw clutch suspension - a hardened and tempered steel spring - an ordinary regulator and an auxiliary one of small weights for delicate adjustments.*

<u>Steel wire ropes</u> *would be used to carry the weights working over large grooved iron pulleys and wrought iron barrels.*

<u>The hammer</u> *for striking the bell would be mounted in an iron frame with steel check spring and bolted to the bell frame in such a manner that the ringing of the bells would not be interfered with.*

<u>The entire cost</u> *of the clock complete and fixed inclusive of all carriage and travelling expenses, clockmakers time during fixing but exclusive of any carpenters or builders work which might be required during fixing would be <u>£58</u> (£3300) a 5'-0" dial with all fittings would be £12 (£680).*

Estimate ll

a clock similar to Estimate l but having an additional "Ding Dong" quarter chimes upon two bells according to the following music would be <u>£84</u> (£4780). (Music)

Estimate lll

a clock similar to Estimate l but having an adaption of "Cambridge" chimes played upon four of the bells according to the following music the cost would be £106 (£6040). (Music)

Should you think well to place any instruction in our care we beg to assure you that they would be carefully carried out to your fullest satisfaction.

                              We beg to Remain
                              Yours obediently
Revd E A Cooke   *John Smith & Sons*
Peasenhall Vicarage
Saxmundham   *P.S. Kindly say if you receive this safely."*

Having obtained estimates a Clock Fund was set up and an issue of the Peasenhall Church Monthly shows that Mr J J Smyth contributed the largest donation of £20 with other substantial donations of £5 each from Capt. Scrivener and Dr. Lay, 10s 6d each from the Earl of Stradbroke and F S Stevenson Esq., M.P., and 2s from Two Friends. On completion of the fund raising a balance sheet was produced:-

"Peasenhall Clock Fund Balance Sheet

Receipts	£.	s.	d.	Expenditure	£.	s.	d.
Balance from Jubilee Fund	4	11	2	J Smith & Sons	70	0	0
Proceeds of Lecture		15	0	Mr H Gibbs	6	0	8
Subscriptions	73	7	0	E Hurren	1	16	0
Bank Interest		3	7	L Pepper		4	6
				Printers A/C		12	6
				Postage		1	1
				Insurance		2	0
	£78	16	9		£78	16	9

Examined and found correct
Francis Tillett, S.A.C.White
Ernest A Cooke, Treasurer
Sept 20th 1899"

The expenditure of £1.16s.0d. to E Hurren, a local builder, was made up of the following:-

	£.	s.	d.
"To myself & Lad & Man & Lad to preparing for Clock & Building Scaffold etc., & making good etc.	1	7	6
Cement 4/9 Mortar 3/-		7	9
Sand			9
	£1	16	0"

John Smith & Sons confirmed by their letter of 24 January 1899 to the Rev. E A Cooke that their estimate of 30 January 1897 still held good, the church clock was erected in April 1899 and the matter was concluded by the following receipt from the clockmakers:-

> "May 1st 1899
> Peasenhall Church Clock Committee
> Bought of John Smith & Sons
> New church clock with 5'-0" dial as per estimate   £70. 0. 0.
> Received with thanks
> May 4th 1899
> John Smith & Sons"

The story is told that during the erection of the clock JJS indicated from an upper window of "Belle View" when the clock was in the correct position on the church tower.

A brass plaque in St Michael's church is inscribed:-

> *The clock in the tower of this church was erected by public subscription to commemorate the 60th anniversary of the accession of Queen Victoria to the throne*

There is also in the church a fine print by Henry Davy of Ipswich dated January 14th 1845 which includes reference to *"Smyth's Drill Manufactory"* and from which the scale of the factory and its physical relationship to the church can be seen.

26 *Photograph of James Josiah Smyth from "Suffolk Celebrities".*
SRO Lowestoft

James Josiah Smyth's inclusion in a *25* book entitled *"Suffolk Celebrities"* by C A Manning Press and published in 1893 illustrates the reputation and high standing he had achieved for the book includes many members of the nobility, members of parliament, justices of the peace, major-generals and other eminent people. His entry in the book is reproduced below:-

"Mr Alderman J.J.Smyth

What - to use a familiar illustration - "Hamlet" would be without the title role, Peasenhall, Suffolk, would be without Mr James Josiah Smyth. He is the life and soul of the place. He is the patron of the living, the proprietor of the Assembly Rooms, an Alderman of the East Suffolk County Council, and an important employer of labour, who delights to live among his people, and manifest a sustained and kindly interest in their welfare. He is managing partner in the firm of Messrs. James Smyth & Sons, drill manufacturers, Peasenhall, with which business he has been connected some forty years. A gentleman of busy brains and great inventive faculty, he is patentee of various improvements in drills, making a speciality of this class of agricultural machinery.

This is an era of mechanical invention, and farming implements have shared in the alterations wrought within the last fifty years. The firm of Messrs. James Smyth & Sons was established as long ago as 1800 - at a period when agriculture was carried on under curiously primitive conditions. Times have changed agriculturally and otherwise, and the firm has changed with them. Mr. J.J.Smyth's inventions have been invaluable in enabling the firm to meet the increasing modern demand for drills of a new and improved type for grain and root crops.

Dean Swift considered that man who could make two ears of corn spring up where only one grew before deserved well of his country. This tribute is essentially Mr. J.J.Smyth's, for what does a good drill do but effect an economy in seeds, and cause the braird to come up more uniformly, and the straw stronger and stiffer?

Mr. Smyth's inventions, then, come as a boon and blessing to farmers in an age which has seen the homely farm of our grandfathers converted into something very much of the nature of a mechanical food factory - thanks to the "kittle o' steam" so contemptuously regarded by Tennyson's "Northern Farmer".

The prosperity of Messrs. James Smyth & Sons is the prosperity of Peasenhall, for our subject is a generous benefactor, commercially and socially, in the neighbourhood. He is interested in its life - its toils and its struggles, its simple enjoyments and its harmless pleasures.

This is altruism peculiarly personal and practical."

Peasenhall had to get used to life without the guiding influence of James Josiah Smyth when, on 26 July 1908, his life came to an end at the age of 75 years. Extracts from his obituary which was published in the *East Anglian Daily Times* of July 29, 1908 are set out below:-

25 SRO Lowestoft

"DEATH OF MR J.J.SMYTH

ROMANCE OF THE PEASENHALL DRILL

Mr. James Josiah Smyth, the head of the well-known firm of drill makers, at Peasenhall, died on Sunday. For many years the name of James Smyth and Peasenhall have been almost synonymous terms. The relationship existing between master and man was so intimate that misunderstandings were very rare, and confidence in each other existed in a marked degree. But the friendships and business connections of Mr Smyth were not confined to the village for which he had done so much. You would travel far to find a man who knew Europe, especially the northern half, better than he did. Educated in Germany, and visiting regularly for many years the important agricultural shows in all the chief centres of Europe, he not only became fully acquainted with the various languages but was cognizant of many of the social events and political aspirations of the people of those countries.

27 The fine memorial in Peasenhall cemetery which marks the final resting place of James Josiah Smyth and his wife Louisa Ann.

26 SRO Ipswich

The Peasenhall Smyths

The late Mr. Smyth was honoured in France in 1889 by being presented with the Cross of "Chevalier du Merite Agricole" for his services to agriculture. For many years he was a member of the Agricultural Engineers Association, and took a lively interest in the various discussions at the meetings.

It must not be forgotten that there have been three persons bearing the name of James Smyth. One died in 1843, another in 1891, while today Peasenhall laments the death of the third.

The late Mr. J.J.Smyth has been connected with the business since 1849, and in 1857 he became a partner. In his time he filled public offices with considerable success. When the East Suffolk County Council was formed in January, 1889, he was elected without opposition to the division of Walpole and was chosen as an Alderman at the first meeting of the Council. As a prominent member of the old Technical Education Committee, he did much to formulate the policy of that body, and spared no effort to make all classes a success, especially those in his own district. He had a great belief in the honour and integrity of the ordinary working man, and desired to place education in all its varied forms well within the reach of all; hoping and trusting in the all wise Providence to guide them aright. For some years he had retired from public life, but formerly he was Chairman of the Liberal Association for the Division of Eye. As Patron of the living of Peasenhall, and an old churchwarden, he took great interest in the Church and its services, but owing to his deafness he was not able in recent years to attend.

The funeral is fixed for tomorrow (Thursday), at 1 p.m., in Peasenhall Cemetery."

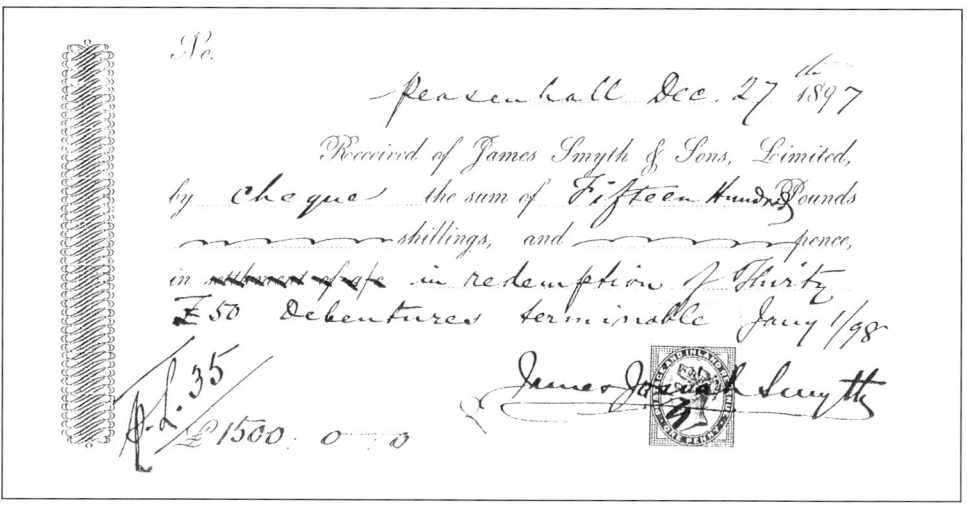

28 Example of James Josiah Smyth's signature.
The value of the cheque equates to about £85,000 at today's value.

James Josiah Smyth had devoted his adult life to the family business which he brought to the height of its prosperity despite the premature loss of his two brothers, he put energy into politics for the betterment of the working man and played a major part in all local affairs where his leadership and generosity were outstanding. With his passing Peasenhall had lost a true friend and supporter.

Sarah Caroline Blackford, the elder sister of JJS, benefited from his *11* will but the main beneficiary was his wife Louisa Ann to whom he bequeathed *"absolutely all my pictures prints books plate linen china liquors household goods furniture chattels and effects and my horse and carriage and I also give to her an annuity of one hundred pounds for her life and absolutely all that my residence known as Belle View situate at Peasenhall aforesaid with the outbuildings gardens orchard and pasture land thereto belonging and also all that small farm with farmhouse and buildings lying to the south of the said residence........."*

Louisa Ann Smyth continued to live at "Belle View" until her death in 1917, she is buried in Peasenhall cemetery with her husband and there the splendid marble monument which marks their grave is inscribed:-

In
Loving Memory of
JAMES JOSIAH SMYTH
who departed this life July 26th 1908
aged 75 years

Also of
LOUISA ANN SMYTH
widow of the above
who died March 12th 1917
aged 84 years

"Not Dead but Sleepeth"
"The Memory of the Just is Blessed"
Prov. X.V.7

A dynasty that for more than one hundred years had made a huge contribution to the life of Peasenhall and left its permanent mark had come to an end.

11 SRO Ipswich

Chapter 5
Memories of Yesteryear

Smyth's were very much a family business and the same was true of its workforce as it was not unusual for several members of one family to be employed at "the Works" and for son to follow father and grandfather often in the same line of work which became a family tradition. Denny, Gardiner, Howard, Paternoster and Rowe feature prominently as Peasenhall families with long associations with the company extending over at least three generations.

The Denny family were renowned as carpenters and wheelwrights with Herbert (known locally as "Nibs") of the second generation earning a high reputation for his skills. When interviewed around 1990 by Mr Tony Martin he said *"I'm Herbert Denny who worked for them (Smyth's) for forty six years and my father sixty years before me"*, he also said *"At seventy I thought I had done enough so I retired when I was seventy in 1965, the day before I left they sold it to the Ross people, they sent in a man who didn't know anything about drills and he couldn't make a success of it so that was the finish of the Smyth works."* He related how the French taxed the drills coming into their country so JJS shipped the drills in parts and sent men to Paris to assemble them thereby avoiding the tax. He also told the story that JJS was doing a job in the village when somebody said to him *"What do the parish think of it?"*; JJS replied *"Well, I am the parish"*! Herbert Denny said *"When I came out of the army in 1919 there was a place for me on the Works, I had other jobs offered but they had applied for me so I started at the Works in 1919."* He went on to say *"When Mr Thirtle was manager there when things got slack we made Scotch carts, we also made sack barrows and other things to keep going. We also made drills to plant maize in South Africa."* No doubt he was referring to the 1920s and 1930s when severe recessions were experienced and Thomas Henry Thirtle was head of the company.

When Herbert Denny retired in 1965 he had given loyal skilled and valuable service for almost half a century.

William Walter Gardiner was born in Sotherton, Suffolk, moving to Peasenhall and then on to Staffordshire. He returned to Peasenhall in about 1903 to work as foreman carpenter at Smyth's where he replaced William George Gardiner following the "Peasenhall Murder". Remarkably, William Walter Gardiner moved into Alma Cottage, The Street, Peasenhall, the cottage previously occupied by the man accused of the murder of Rose Harsent. Two of William Walter Gardiner's five sons, Fred and Tom followed their father into the carpenter's shop at "the Works", with a third, Albert, employed in the foundry and later in the paint shop. Albert's son Herbert, continued the family tradition of working in the carpenter's shop where he earned his living from 1943 to the closure of the business in 1967.

Eric Howard started working for Smyth's on leaving school in 1940; he worked in the fitting shop until 1943 when he joined the Royal Navy, returning in 1947 following demobilisation to resume his work in the fitting shop and later in the tin shop. In 1960, when his weekly wage was nine pounds and ten shillings, he foresaw the end of the company and left to obtain more secure employment. Eric Howard's brother Frank worked in the blacksmiths' shop.

29 Charlie Howard in 1911 when he was chauffeur to the Collett family who lived at Peasenhall Hall. The photograph was taken at the Ancient House, Peasenhall.

Charles Howard, the father of Eric and Frank, worked initially as a chauffeur for the Collett family who had acquired The Hall in 1892 following the death of James Smyth jnr. but, on demobilisation from the Army Service Corps at the end of the First World War, he was employed by Smyth's as their lorry driver. He and his family lived in the factory site house, part of which served as the company offices, and he retired in 1962.

Charles Howard's brothers, William, Harold and Albert worked in the foundry, as did two of William's three sons, George and John. Charles Howard's father, also Charles, spent his working life in Smyth's foundry.

For many years the fortunes of the Howard family were closely linked to the prosperity or otherwise of "the Works".

George Howard, referred to above, on leaving school in 1937 when he was fourteen years old started work as an apprentice core maker and moulder in Smyth's foundry but shortage of work caused him to leave in early 1940 and he completed his apprenticeship at Garrett's of Leiston. He joined the Royal Navy in 1941 and on demobilisation in 1946 he returned to Smyth's to work in the foundry. When interviewed recently he described the work as hot and dusty, explaining that it would take two or three days to fill the floor of the foundry with moulds then for one or two days a week the metal would be melted and poured into the moulds. He also confirmed that during the difficult times before the Second World War the foundry made castings for other firms including many cooking ranges for R J Pryce & Co. a leading firm of Lowestoft ironmongers.

George Howard also described how the staff "clocked on and off" by means of a key which registered the individual's personal number and how on pay day (Friday) they would go to the office where each employee's weekly wage had been put in a tin marked with his personal number; the contents of the tin would be checked and the tin left in the office for the next pay day.

Another feature of life at Smyth's, and in this case the entire village, was the works hooter which sounded at 7.45am, 8am, 12noon, 1pm and 5pm; the hooter always gave one long and two short blasts and for many years was sounded by one William "Tich" Kemp.

George Howard recalled how he enjoyed working at Smyth's as those employed there knew each other and this created a family atmosphere, unlike Garrett's, which being a much larger business, was somewhat impersonal and unfriendly.

The first known generation of Paternosters to work at the factory were the brothers Billy, who worked in the timber mill, and Charlie who was employed in the fitting shop. Billy's three sons, Herbert (paint shop), Albert (paint shop) and Stanley James (blacksmith) followed their father to his place of work. Stanley's son, Stanley William, took after his father by working for Smyth's and carrying on the skills of a blacksmith. Ronnie Paternoster, Stanley William's cousin, worked in the timber yard for many years and another cousin, Cynthia Paternoster, spent a few years in the company office towards the end of the company's existence.

Fred Rowe was company secretary for many years and this makes his recorded comments when interviewed by Mr Tony Martin particularly informative and valuable. He confirmed that he started work in the office on his fourteenth birthday in 1917 when he earned six shillings a week; five people worked in the office at that time and there was no telephone or a typewriter. He said that Smyth's employed about fifty or sixty workers when he started but with the bad times of the 1920s they had to get rid of several (his words). They (Smyth's) did not make munitions or armaments in either of the World Wars, making only drills in the First World War and during the Second World War they got big orders from the government. When he started some workers earned about one pound a week, others about two pounds. There were two main agents - one in Holland and one in France.

He said *"There were no Smyths when I went there. The last Smyth died about*

30 A job well done by Stanley Paternoster a Works blacksmith.

1908, Josiah, and he never had any children." He went on to say that Mr Blackford was the boss when he started followed by Mr Thirtle, they were both nephews of JJS, and Mr Thirtle married a niece of JJS. Smyth's used a great deal of paint and Fred Rowe described that they made their own paint by buying red lead and white lead and mixed it up - mixed the colours they wanted.

Confirmation of the difficult times and reasons for the decline of the business were provided when he said *"We had lots of slack times and never knew if it was going to survive or not. But you see after Mr Smyth died they hadn't another with his brain - you see neither Mr Blackford or Mr Thirtle had been in the agricultural business - they weren't mechanically minded and couldn't invent anything new - we never moved with the times."*

He said that in good times about three hundred drills were made in a year, there were two makes of drills - the Nonpareil and the Eclipse, the first Nonpareil was made about 1870 and in Essex they made an all wood lever drill called a semi-Nonpareil (the reference to Essex no doubt meant the Witham works). Local farmers occasionally came to the works to buy a drill but most were sold through agents - there were agencies all over England.

Talking about the decline and demise of the business he remarked *"There was a fire in 1923 - more than half the place was destroyed - it was wondered at the time if it was going to be rebuilt. They started to go behind after the First World War -*

then during the 1920s there was a slack period - then it was the same for a time during the 1930s. They came on again during the 1939 war because there was a demand for their drills. The drills were probably too well made and lasted for too long - they were also repaired which extended their life. When I finished Mr Scrivener was there and he sold out to the Ross Group. Johnson was in charge of the Ross Agricultural Division. Ransomes had the spares for a time."

The final quote typifies the continuity of employment at "the Works" experienced by many Peasenhall families:- *"My father was on there and my grandfather worked there as well - my father wanted me to go on. My father was a moulder. My grandfather went around demonstrating drills a lot all over the country."*

Having regard to the long period of employment at Smyth's (from 1917 until the 1960s) and his many years as company secretary which enabled him to have an overview of all aspects of the business and become familiar with its history, the comments made by Fred Rowe provide invaluable information and confirmation on aspects of the business and its history where there is a paucity of documentary evidence or none at all.

Fred Rowe was one of many members of his family to work at the Church Street site; it is known from his own remarks that his father, Herbert, and a grandfather worked there before him, to which can be added Fred's brother, Will, who was employed in the fitting shop. Will's daughter, Brenda, worked in the company office from 1942 to 1962 and she married Raymond ("Bunty") Newson who also worked in the office during the period 1941-1962. Herbert Rowe's cousin, Charles Rowe, worked at the factory as a foreman (department not known) and of his sons at least four were employed at Smyth's, Albert (tin shop), Jesse (foundryman), Leonard (carpenters' shop) and Edgar (paint shop); Jesse was severely injured in the First World War and, although he survived, his injuries prevented him returning to Smyth's. Edgar Rowe's son, Jim, also worked as a foundryman.

A small army of Rowe's earned their living at "the Works".

Reggie Friend was the third ex-employee who was interviewed by Mr Tony Martin and some of his statements give an interesting insight into working arrangements and conditions. He started the interview by saying *"My father worked there fifty years and my grandfather before him. I worked in the blacksmith's shop all the while. We did all the fitting in the blacksmith's shop years ago - the fitting shop used to do the lathe work but we used to do all the fitting in the blacksmith's shop. I wasn't a blacksmith although I was as good as one - I was a blacksmith's striker and fitter. I used to swing a sixteen pounds hammer from 6.30 in the morning until 6 at night all day"* He started in 1916 when he was sixteen years old - *"you couldn't get on there before."* He described that there were fourteen fires on the go all day and two steam hammers in the blacksmith's shop. *"There were twenty two men working in the blacksmith's shop when I first went there. I got paid ten bob a week when I first went there - if you were a good boy you got another two bob but it was a long time before you got any more. When I first worked there Smyth's made everything, every mortal thing including little nuts and bolts - things were made odd sizes so no one else could supply them.*" The last comment illustrates the shrewdness of the company in ensuring they had the monopoly of all spares which could be supplied only by them. Reggie Friend continued *"After the First World War they lost the French trade* (This is not strictly correct). *When Josiah died they lacked an engineer because he was a good engineer;"* he went on to describe JJS as *"a rum old cup of tea"* but this remark could not have been based on first hand knowledge as he was only eight years old when JJS died in 1908. Describing the conditions during the Great Depression he said *"During the 1930s - this was during the depression - we worked a week on and a week off - during this time they also made wheelbarrows and tumbrels but they were too dear."* The comparative attraction of working at Smyth's is illustrated by his comment that *"Men on "the Works" got better pay than agricultural workers and also had Saturday afternoon and Sunday off."*

He said there were about ninety eight workers there and over one hundred if the office staff were included (these numbers do not accord with those given by Fred Rowe); the old drills were called Eclipse then they made Nonpareil; after they made the Nonpareil about 1880 they still made the Eclipse until about 1918 or 1920.

Reggie Friend concluded the interview with a fascinating story:-

"There were two foremen on "the Works" - one in charge of all woodwork and one in charge of all ironwork. The one in charge of all ironwork when I was there was old Cook who used to live on the Causeway. He was over six foot tall and used to wear one of those pork pie hats which used to make him look about seven foot. Didn't know how much he weighed - about sixteen or seventeen stone. They made his coffin on "the Works" in the carpenter's shop and when they done that three men got inside of it - Tom Gardiner, Fred Gardiner and Fred Smith. He (Cook) lived on the Causeway and they couldn't get the coffin out of the door and they had to take out the whole frame out of the window and got the coffin out of the window. He was as strong as a blinking "hoss", have seen him bend the vice pin but he could neither read nor write. He was over the blacksmith's shop, the tin shop and the foundry. The other one was over the paint shop and the carpenter's shop - he was Gardiner."

"Old Cook" appears to have been quite a character and not a man with whom to pick an argument!

For many years it was the custom and practice for Smyth's to make the coffin for a deceased employee or a member of his family and one inch boards of oak were prepared for this purpose.

Before mains electricity was supplied to the factory the power was provided by a steam engine which ran off two boilers and this produced all the motive power and lighting, to be followed by a Lister ex-wartime searchlight generator and a large Lister diesel engine which ran the saw mill.

Raymond ("Bunty") Newson was another former employee who was able to give valuable information particularly about the period of the Second World War. He started work at Smyth's in February 1941 and left in June 1962 to take up other employment as he could see the serious problems building up.

He was employed as a sales ledger and dispatch clerk and shared the company offices with Frank Thirtle (managing director), Fred Rowe (company secretary), and his wife Brenda (nee Rowe) who was Fred Rowe's niece. He confirmed that during the Second World War, in order to cope with increased orders and the shortage of some skilled workers on active service, the company brought in castings from ironfounders such as Diss Foundry Ltd., East Dereham Foundry and H N Rumsby and Sons, Waveney iron works, Bungay. Wheels for the drills were made by Boast of Rendham, B W Quinton and Fred Thirkettle both of Laxfield, Suffolk; some shoeing of the wheels was done by Hector Moore, a Brandeston blacksmith.

The country was fighting for its survival and this was a time for using all possible resources to maintain output of agricultural implements that would contribute to the production of food. Sadly, Raymond Newson died in July 2002.

Returning to the Friend family, Olive Borrett, the sister of Reggie Friend and one of Peasenhall's most senior residents, has personal memories of the devastating fire at the Peasenhall site in 1923 for at that time her family lived in one of the firm's cottages in Church Street which, because they were at risk from fire spread, were evacuated and their contents stored at the nearby "Ancient House"; Olive recounts the story that she returned home from spending some time during the school holidays with an aunt and uncle to find her school books among the items removed from the cottage and she wished they had been destroyed as she was due to return to school on the following Monday and the work in her school books wasn't too good! She also remembers the firm's lorries taking the young children who attended Sunday school to Dunwich for a treat.

Mrs Borrett did munitions work at Ransomes of Ipswich during the Second World War and during that war she also worked in the blacksmiths' shop at Smyth's. Other women who worked at Smyth's during the Second World War included Hilda Nichols, Jean Nichols (later Paternoster), Marjorie Chorlton, Gladys Teago, Mabel Woodard, and Brenda Rowe (later Newson).

Now for a few words about a man who was something of a "character" and who probably typifies the reliable, loyal and hard-working man who earned his living at Smyth's. Fred Burgess is the man and the information concerning him is based on the diaries that he maintained and the personal knowledge of his daughter, Mrs Chilvers of Framlingham, Suffolk. Fred Burgess was adopted as a child by Mrs W Harper of Casey Court, Peasenhall and he did not know his parents or his date of birth; on leaving school at about the age of fourteen years he was at first employed as a telegram boy before becoming a postman on 31 July 1899; in one of his diaries he recorded the people to whom he delivered telegrams including prominent people like the Smyths, the Colletts of Peasenhall Hall, a Colonel Wards and Lord Huntingfield of Heveningham, Suffolk. He also recorded *"The new clock was started on Thursday evening at eight o'clock by Mrs J J Smyth April 1899";* clearly a reference to the new clock on the tower of St Michael's church, Peasenhall. He joined in 1909 the 4th battalion of the Suffolk Regiment as a territorial soldier and served with that unit during the First World War (1914-1918) being wounded in 1915 during the fighting at Neuve Chapelle, was hospitalised in Yorkshire before returning to the Western Front. His army records show that he was born in Peasenhall on 10 December 1884, although that is by no means certain and his commanding officer giving a character reference in 1916 said *"I consider him a very steady, capable and industrious man, and well able to fill a position of trust."*

Fred Burgess joined Smyth's in the early 1900s from where he retired in the late 1950s having given something in the order of fifty years service. He was employed as a painter and fitter and he would often accompany the drills to various agricultural shows; on one occasion he nearly caused an industrial dispute - one of the drills for display had been slightly damaged during transport and Fred duly got out his paint and brushes to do some "touching up" of the damaged area - painters employed at the building where the show was being held were staunch members of a trade union (which Fred wasn't) and they took exception to non-union labour doing their "work" - Fred stopped his painting, waited for the trade unionists to leave work and then got on with his painting!

It would be remiss to close this chapter without some reference to Frank Thirtle who headed the company for more than twenty years. Frank Elven Thirtle born around the turn of the 19th century, the eldest son of Thomas Henry Thirtle of Lowestoft, married in 1935 Gwen who was born in Lowestoft of Welsh parents and they lived at "Apple Tree Cottage", Middleton, Suffolk; it was said that the cottage was the first property in Middleton to have electricity, which was powered from a Lister engine charging fifty six batteries giving 110 volts direct current, and also was the first to have a telephone. He drove the five miles or so to the Peasenhall factory and each day came home for lunch!

Frank Thirtle in effect took over the running of the business on the death of his father in 1938, although probably he had been doing this for some time before then and, following the period of the Second World War when it was necessary to use great initiative to overcome the shortage of skilled men and other resources, it fell to him to oversee the difficult times of the 1950s when Smyth's simply did not have the resources or infra-structure of a scale necessary to compete in the post-war world as technological developments and changes in industrial and agricultural practices took effect leaving Smyth's in their wake. He died at the early age of 61 years in 1961 and it is possible that the pressures of managing the business during the previous decade contributed to his sudden death.

Frank Thirtle was a leading member of the community in Middleton and served for many years on the parish council. He was elected a parish councillor and signed a declaration of office on 18 April 1942; he was elected chairman of the parish council and signed a declaration of office on 26 April 1947. He continued to serve as a parish councillor and attended his last meeting on 30 May 1961 - the next meeting was held on 10 October 1961 and the minutes of the meeting state:- *"The Chairman asked all present to stand in silence as a tribute to the memory of the late Mr F Thirtle. The Chairman paid tribute to Mr Thirtle's work on the council and stated a wreath had been sent on behalf of the Members. The council agreed that a letter of condolence be sent to Mrs Thirtle."* The minutes record *"Colonel H Gordon Dean in the Chair."*

The man who had led Smyth's for more than twenty years died on 2 August 1961 and he was cremated at Ipswich crematorium on 8 August; the records at the crematorium show that Frank Thirtle's ashes were taken to Lowestoft, where it is believed they were intended to be scattered in the churchyard at St Margaret's church, but that they were returned to Ipswich crematorium where they were scattered in the Garden of Rest.

People who knew Frank Thirtle over many years describe him as a *"lovely friendly man"* and there is little doubt that he had a good relationship with the workforce, would help anybody if he could, and did his utmost for the benefit of the business and those whose livelihood depended on it.

An extract from the minutes of a meeting of Middleton parish council on 9 December 1958 reflects Frank Thirtle's helpful and friendly nature:- *"The Clerk reported that after the last Council Meeting Mr Thirtle had very kindly offered to lend his typewriter for Council work. The typewriter had been repaired and is satisfactory. The Council expressed their appreciation and thanks to Mr Thirtle."*

Frank Thirtle was a true gentleman.

The individuals mentioned in this final chapter are only a small selection of an army of people whose working lives revolved around a business which made such a large contribution to the life of a small community and this story closes with the belief that Smyth's will continue to hold an important place in the history of Peasenhall, a community whose village sign most appropriately features a seed drill.

Appendix A

Peasenhall Mechanics' Institute and Reading Room

<< RULES >>

1ST. - That this Society be called THE PEASENHALL MECHANICS' INSTITUTE AND READING ROOM.

2ND. - That the Officers of the Society consist of President, Vice-President, Secretary, Treasurer and a Committee of nine members, who shall be elected annually.

3RD. - That the Committee be solely responsible for the management and order of the room, and that they shall in turn be in attendance one night each in the week to maintain order. The Committee man's decision to be final on all points.

4TH. - That the Subscription of members be Sixpence per month, to be paid in advance.

5TH. - That the subscription of lady members be Three Shillings per year (payable quarterly in advance), which will entitle them to the use of the room from 11 a.m. to 5 p.m.

6TH. - That members whose subscriptions are three months in arrears must pay within seven days from receiving notice or be expelled.

7TH. - That the room be open every day from 11 a.m. to 10 p.m.

8TH. - That every candidate for admission must be over 18 years of age and must be proposed by any member, and his name to be placed on the notice board one week before admission.

9TH. - That no smoking be allowed in the room before 6 p.m.

10TH. - That during the month of January a General Meeting shall be held for the purpose of electing new Officers and passing Accounts.

Appendix B

RULES
of the
Drill Manufactory
BENEFIT SOCIETY
held at the
PEASENHALL
MECHANICS' INSTITUTE

~~~~~~~~~~~~~~~~~

1865

~~~~~~~~~~~~~~~

Drill Manufactory Benefit Society
PEASENHALL

~~~~~~~~~~~~~~~~~~~~~~~

RULE I.
This Society shall be known as the "Drill Manufactory Benefit Society".

RULE II.
That the object of this Society shall be to render assistance during sickness or accident.

RULE III.
That every man or boy in Messrs. Smyth & Sons' employ, not already entitled to assistance from any other Benefit Society, will be expected to join this Society, and in event of his neglecting so to do, he is distinctly to understand that in case of illness, no subscription will be allowed to be made on his behalf.

RULE IV.
That the affairs of this Society be under the management of a Chairman, Treasurer and six Stewards.

RULE V.
That the duty of the Chairman shall be, to preside at all the meetings and to give the casting vote when necessary. The Chairman to be elected at each meeting from the Members then present.

RULE VI.
That the duty of the Treasurer shall be to receive all monies and to make such payments as the Acting-Stewards may direct.

RULE VII.
That of the six Stewards, two shall be Acting-Stewards, that the Acting-Stewards will hold Office for one-quarter of a year, and upon retiring, their Office shall be

filled by two other of the Stewards in the order of their election, and that the two new Stewards be elected at each Quarterly Meeting, and that the duties of the Acting-stewards shall be:-

To receive applications for sick allowance.

To issue written instructions to Treasurer to make all necessary payments.

To visit sick Members once every week, (and should the sick Member live more than two miles from the Manufactory receive threepence for every mile over two miles but in no case to be expected to go more than six miles from the Manufactory).

To be present at all Meetings.

To enlist new comers.

To watch over the interests of the Society in general.

To Audit the Accounts previous to retiring from Office.

And that in event of one or both Acting-Stewards being unable to fulfil their duties his or their Office shall be filled by other Stewards in order of their election.

RULE VIII.
That in event of either or both Acting-Stewards being absent from the Quarterly Meetings, he or they shall be fined One Shilling each; the fine to go to the Funds of the Society.

RULE IX.
That in event of both Stewards neglecting to visit the sick each week; he whose turn it shall have been, shall be fined Sixpence, the same to go to the Fund.

RULE X.
That a General Quarterly Meeting of the Members be held on the first Wednesday in the months of January, April, July and October, (at the MECHANICS' INSTITUTE between the hours of 7.30 and 9 o'Clock p.m.) for the purpose of electing Stewards, Auditing Accounts and the transaction of any business which may arise.

RULE XI.
That no Member under the age of 18 years, shall have any voice in the management of the Society's affairs, nor fill any Office.

RULE XII.
That all matters of dispute shall be settled by the Vote of majority at Meeting assembled.

RULE XIII.
That if any member quarrels with or abuses another during Club hours, he shall forfeit the sum of One Shilling to the Fund.

RULE XIV.
That in event of three or more Members deeming it necessary (at any time) to convene a Special Meeting, the Acting Stewards shall at their written request convene such Meeting.

RULE XV.
That this Society shall consist of Four Classes of Members:-

Class l.   Monthly Subscription 4d. Full allowance during sickness 4d. per day.
Class ll. Monthly Subscription 8d. Full allowance during sickness 8d. per day.
Class lll. Monthly Subscription 1s. Full allowance during sickness 1s. per day.
Class IV. Monthly Subscription 1s.4d. Full allowance during sickness 1s.4d. per day.

RULE XVI.
That the Class to which a Member may Subscribe shall be at the discretion of the Stewards, and who may not exceed the restriction of Rule XXI.

RULE XVII.
That Full-Pay shall continue no longer than 12 weeks, and after that term, Half-Pay which shall not continue longer than 12 months.

RULE XVIII.
That in event of any Member falling sick within 26 weeks of his having been on the Funds of the Society, he shall be placed in the same situation as when he ceased receiving his sick allowance.

RULE XIX.
That no sick pay shall be allowed, unless a Doctor's or Chemist's note is delivered to one of the Acting Stewards.

RULE XX.
That in order to be entitled to the sick pay for the day upon which the Medical Note is received by the Acting Stewards; such Note must be delivered before 12 o'Clock at noon.

RULE XXI.
That no Member shall belong to a Class, in which, in case of sickness, he shall receive more than three-fourths of his usual day wages when at work.

RULE XXII.
That no Member shall be entitled to sick pay, unless he has been a Member for six weeks.

RULE XXIII.
That each Member by joining this Society consents to his Subscription being taken from his wages, (at Messrs. SMYTH & SONS' OFFICE) monthly in advance.

RULE XXIV.
That each Member's interest in this Society ceases upon his leaving Messrs. SMYTH & SONS' employ.

RULE XXV.
That any sick Member living more than six miles from the Drill Manufactory shall send to one of the Acting Stewards a Medical Note weekly.

RULE XXVI.
That no undue advantage shall be taken of a sick Member; but the Rules shall be liberally construed where no fraudulent intention appears, nevertheless should any Member receive an accident by fighting, wrestling or any dangerous practice or bravado, he shall receive no Sick allowance, nor for the venereal disease. And should a sick Member be found drinking to excess, offering to fight, or doing that which is likely to retard his recovery, or be found more than 2 miles from home or out later than 8 o'Clock in the evening from Lady-day to Michaelmas-day, or 5 o'Clock in the evening from Michaelmas-day to Lady-day he shall be fined One shilling for each offence should the Stewards think fit.

RULE XXVII.
That in event of a sick Member being found at work whilst receiving sick allowance he shall be fined Twenty Shillings.

RULE XXVIII.
That in event of a Member of this Society dying his survivors shall receive towards funeral expenses according to the following scale:-

Class I. Ten Shillings.

Class II. Twenty Shillings.

Class III. Thirty Shillings.

Class IV. Forty Shillings.

The same to be raised by a special subscription among the Members of this Society in the ratio of their Monthly subscriptions.

RULE XXIX.
That each Member shall be entitled to a Book of Rules on payment of Threepence.

RULE XXX.
That no addition or alteration shall be made to these Rules, except at the wish of a majority of Members (entitled to a vote), at a Special Meeting convened for that purpose. Made this 1st day of February, 1865, in Meeting assembled.

JAMES JOSIAH SMYTH, Chairman.

Appendix C

Key Dates

1800 Business founded by James Smyth snr.

1840 James Smyth jnr. sole proprietor of the business.

1843 James Smyth snr. dies 12 December aged 66 years.

1844 – 1848 Smyth's start operations in Witham, Essex.

1857 James Josiah Smyth, eldest son of James Smyth jnr., becomes partner and manager of the business.

1860 Earliest known reference to a Smyth depot in France (Dieppe).

1868 Smyth's continental depot now in Paris.

1891 James Smyth jnr. dies 8 December aged 84 years.

1893 Smyth's become a registered company with James Josiah and his brother Ralph Alexander Mac Smyth the principal shareholders.

1894 Monsieur Jules Gontier appointed manager of the Paris warehouse.

1896 Witham operations close.

1907 Paris warehouse vacated and M. Gontier appointed general agent for France.

1908 James Josiah Smyth dies 26 July aged 75 years.

1918 James Smyth Blackford dies 27 December aged 53 years.

1923 Devastating fire at Peasenhall factory 30 August.

1938 Thomas Henry Thirtle dies 2 August aged 68 years.

1961 Frank Elven Thirtle dies 2 August aged 61 years.

1962 Company taken over by John Levett-Scrivener and Alec Stearn.

1965 Business bought by Ross Group of Grimsby.

1967 Business closes 30 April.

Bibliography

"Ransomes of Ipswich. A History of the Firm and a Guide to its Records"
by D R Grace and D C Phillips
University of Reading 1975

"Garretts of Leiston"
by R A Whitehead 1964

"The Collett Saga"
by Margaret Chadd 1988

"East Anglia's First Railways"
by Hugh Moffatt 1987

"A Survey of the Agriculture of Suffolk"
by P J O Trist 1971

"The Smyth Family of Swefling and Peasenhall, Suffolk - with particular reference to Jonathan Smyth"
Paper by Rod Crook Hobart Australia 2001